INTRODUCTION TO THE STURNEY FAMILY LETTERS

Imagine finding an old leather book with a dusty smell and a well-worn cover. As you look inside it you see pictures of your parents when they were young. As you flick the pages you see more photos – one that says it's of your dad and older brother who in this photo is a baby in his father's arms. I was probably a young teenager when I first came across the book and the other two that accompanied it. I remember being told by my parents that it had been made by Grandpa Sturney, who I knew had a hobby of book binding. They told me it was made up of photos and letters they had sent to him and my nana when they lived in the Cook Islands, the country of my birth. Then the book disappeared for a few years, probably hidden away from prying eyes and grubby fingers.

It wasn't until five or six years later that I was allowed to read it, and what I read blew me away. It wasn't so much a dramatic read but an enlightening one. For the first time I read about the everyday life of my parents in the islands – starting with their journey out in 1958. I read about my brother Marcus as he transitioned from being a baby into a toddler and then young child. I read about the houses we lived in, Dad's job, the missionary society and church organisation – the Cook Islands Christian Church – he worked for and in. There were some funny stories as well as some sad ones. Then, for the first time I read about my traumatic birth and the depth of my parents' faith. I had heard some stories before but not in this amount of detail. In those days you couldn't make a simple phone call or send a text message, record a voice note or send an email, there was no social media and very little info in the public domain about the Cook Islands. So every letter my grandparents received was central to their understanding of what life was like for their son, daughter-in-law and grandsons.

When we set out on a journey, we don't always know what our final destination will look like. That's how it was for my dad John (aged 27), my mum Rita (aged 28) and my brother Marcus who was ten months old. Dad had not long been ordained as a

Congregational Minister (now United Reformed Church) and married to Mum for a couple of years when he felt the call to become a missionary with the London Missionary Society (L.M.S.). At the end of Dad's missionary training the board invited him and his friend to a meeting where they told them where they were going to be deployed. His friend was to go to the Cook Islands and he was to go to Madagascar. Dad said to his friend, "You are associated with the Boy Scouts and they are in Madagascar, and I'm associated with the Boys' Brigade and they are in the Cook Islands, let's ask to swap." So they went back to the board and they agreed to them swapping. When Dad began his journey to become a missionary he was unaware of where he was to be deployed and after a twist ended up in the Cook Islands. That swap began an amazing journey of destiny, discovery and now legacy.

As a family we have often wondered what others would make of our story. At one level it is just a simple account of everyday life for a young family living and working on the other side of the world, over 60 years ago. But of course it is more than that; it is an historic account of life in the Cook Islands, the role of a young missionary sent by the L.M.S. and the early years of the Cook Islands Christian Church – which remains the largest church in the islands. As you read it I hope you'll enjoy this three-year journey with us. Sadly, we have none of the letters from the second three years, when the family returned to the islands after a break back in England. However, we have some photos from the next few years which have been included. I'm sure some of you will marvel, as I do, at the change in the islands over the 60 years. Faces in the photographs have aged as have many of the buildings, but the palm tree still sways in the gentle breeze, stories continue to be told and memories made. Incredibly Dad is still alive at 93 and able to tell his stories, share his memories and thoughts.

The letters are a legacy left to shine a light on what life was like for this young missionary family. They also show the legacy left by the L.M.S., which gave birth to the Cook Islands Christian Church. And lastly they are a family legacy, something our family for generations to come can delve into and learn about their connections with the islands.

Thank you for joining us on our journey – Simeon Sturney (2025)

the Sturney Family

INTRODUCTION TO THE COOK ISLANDS

Great Polynesian Migration

Cook Islanders are true Polynesians connecting directly back to the finest seafarers of the Pacific. Sophisticated navigation took them fearlessly in search of new lands. From 1500 bc Polynesian islands were gradually populated by Maori ancestors who landed in their *vakas* (magnificent giant double-hulled canoes) guided by the stars and their famous power of navigation. The Cook Islands stretch out in a scattering of 2 million square kilometres. Polynesians arrived in Rarotonga around 800 ad, sailing from Tupua'i, now French Polynesia.

The Maori migrations to New Zealand began from Rarotonga as early as the 5th century ad. Closely linked in culture and language to the Maori in New Zealand, the Maohi of French Polynesia, the Rapanui of Easter Island and the Kanaka Maoli of Hawaii – about 87 percent of Cook Islanders are Polynesian Cook Island Maori.

Captain James Cook

After stopovers from Spanish explorers Alvaro de Mendana sighting Pukapuka in 1595, and Pedro Fernandez de Quiros sighting Rakahanga in 1606, Captain James Cook sighted Manuae in 1773, then subsequently Palmerston, Takutea, Mangaia and Atiu, where Lieutenant Gore landed in 1777. The redoubtable Captain William Bligh first sighted Aitutaki in 1789 and soon after, following the very bloody mutiny on the *Bounty*, the buccaneer Fletcher Christian, having seconded Captain Bligh's very own boat, sailed into Rarotonga.

Christian Missionaries

The influence of the first Christian missionaries in 1821 was immediate. Their arrival altered the traditional way of life, yet the Cook Islanders have managed to beautifully preserve their proud Polynesian heritage and blend it with their Christian faith. Aitutaki was the first island of the Cook Islands to accept Christianity so in 1823 a limestone coral rock church was built in Arutanga and is the oldest church in the Cook Islands. The stunning acoustics of CICC make for a moving experience. The influence of the missionaries has been of benefit to all, with the beautiful white churches, the acapella singing on Sundays and the traditional *muumuu* coming from them.

Political History

Originally named the Hervey Isles after a British lord, the Russians named them the Cook Islands in honour of the famous captain in 1823.

In 1901 New Zealand decided to annex the country. Many of the islands were independently ruled by local chiefs with no federal statutory law to decide such things. However, it remained a protectorate until 1965, when as a self-governing state under New Zealand's auspices, Sir Albert Henry was elected Prime Minister. Today the country is essentially self-governing in free association with New Zealand, which oversees defence.

Information provided by www.cookislands.travel

THE MISSIONARIES OF THE LONDON MISSIONARY SOCIETY WHO HAVE SERVED IN THE COOK ISLANDS

REV. JOHN WILLIAMS	1823-1839
REV. CHARLES PITMAN	1827-1854
REV. AARON BUZACOTT	1828-1857
REV. WILLIAM GILL	1839-1852
REV. HENRY ROYLE	1839-1876
REV. GEORGE GILL	1845-1860
REV. WYATT GILL	1852-1863
REV. ERNEST KRAUSE	1859-1867
REV. JAMES CHALMERS	1867-1877
REV. GEORGE HARRIS	1871-1893
REV. JOHN HUTCHIN	1882-1912
REV. WILLIAM LAURENCE	1884-1905
MISS ARDILL	1892-1898
REV. JAMES CULLEN	1894-1902
MISS LARGE	1895-1902
REV. PERCY HALL	1900-1916
REV. JOHN JONES	1901-1905
REV. BOND JAMES	1902-1934
REV. GEORGE EASTMAN	1913-1918
REV. HERBERT BRALSFORD	1927-1930
REV. HENRY CATER	1931-1943
REV. ROBERT CHALLIS	1933-1947
REV. WILLIAM MURPHY	1947-1956
REV. BERNARD THOROGOOD	1956-1963
REV. JOHN STURNEY	1958-1965
REV. JOHN F. CLERKE	1964-1967
REV. BERNARD THOROGOOD	1968-1970
REV. B.G. BEALING	1972-1974

ACKNOWLEDGEMENTS

Reaching our destiny is often a journey supported by others. It was the case for my parents, who had many people and organisations supporting them during their time in the Cook Islands. Likewise, there have been many people involved in the journey of this book. I'm grateful to Dad and my brother Marcus for giving permission for these letters to be published – after all, many of them were private thoughts my parents committed to paper, in order to invite Dad's parents into their physical, emotional and spiritual journey. Mum and Dad have left the family an amazing legacy which we will treasure. The family is indebted to our grandfather A.C. Sturney, who had the foresight to not only keep the letters but have them typed and made into the first collection of letters – accompanied by photos and other documents.

For years my family have dreamt of getting these original "scrapbooks", three volumes, published. We are grateful to Sarah Grace and Malcolm Down at Grace & Down Publishing for taking on this project. From the moment Sarah saw the original volumes she has championed this venture – thank you. It's one thing to have a concept and raw material, it is quite another to bring it all to life; this has been expertly done by Faye Porter at Bubble Designs. She has blended the letters, photos and documents and added a thematic graphic design which brings everything together and invites the onlooker to join the journey. Thank you so much.

There are a whole host of other people to thank – family, friends and others who have contributed in various ways, including professionally and financially, to this wonderful outcome, a huge thank you to you all.
Simeon Sturney – 2025.

DISCLAIMER

The letters you are about to read weren't written to be published or to be read by anyone other than the people they were addressed to. Each letter may have been written over a few days or even a week or two. Some were handwritten and some typed on a very old typewriter. No copies were kept by those writing them, so the writer couldn't always remember what they had written in a previous letter. They were written over 60 years ago, in a very different era, with different technologies and a different way of phrasing things. The language used was indicative of the cultural background of the writer and in no way meant to cause consternation or confusion. We have been careful when editing the letters to keep the original intent, syntax and in most cases the same phraseology. However, a few minor alterations have been made in order to clarify anything that may not be understood in today's "world" and in some cases a few letters grouped together under one main heading. We also note that some customs and wording has changed in the Cook Islands over the years. For example, we now refer to the cyclone season and not hurricane season, alcohol is now no longer prohibited, there are of course many hotels, resorts and holiday homes widely available on Rarotonga and Aitutaki. The Nuku – Gospel Day – is also widely celebrated on various islands and at different times in the year, as opposed to only on Rarotonga, when these letters were written. Throughout the letters Dad refers to Europeans, which was a generic term for white people or foreigners. With this understanding, we hope you enjoy reading a little of our family history, the culture of the period and the day-to-day life of a missionary and family sent to the other side of the world, where the pace of life and infrastructure was very different from everything they had known before. Thank you for picking up this book, and sharing in our story.

Legacy

A Missionary's Life
Letters from the Cook Islands / Kuki Airani

Extracts from letters written by the Rev. John Sturney & Mrs Rita Sturney

Farewell at Tilbury

LETTERS FROM SEPTEMBER 1958 – THE OUTBOUND JOURNEY

DEPARTURE FROM TILBURY
Our first letter to you on this long first stage of our journey to our new home. Had strange thoughts come into my mind when I think of the many other letters we shall write through the years!

I really didn't want the boat to go as it slid away from the dockside at Tilbury, even though a few minutes before I had been hoping that it would go quickly. We felt a bit weatherbeaten and worn when we eventually lost sight of you and returned to our cabin. But I think it was easier for us than for you, having Marcus to worry about.

FIRST IMPRESSIONS ON BOARD SHIP
Unfortunately all the young raw stewards are in the children's dining room so his first meal was not a great success; they'd just no idea what a ten-month-old baby should have. However, most of these troubles are now over and he is able to have a much more normal routine meal. We both came away hungry after our first meal – I even more so, for I ordered, mistakenly, an appetiser as my main dish!

The afternoon was spent in sorting our cases and unpacking and generally finding our whereabouts. The evening meal became more lively. We sat at a table with a couple returning home to New Zealand and found they were the people who Auntie and Uncle had suggested we look out for. Small world, isn't it.

Suddenly the sea didn't seem so big nor our ship so small.

We had to put the clocks back 84 minutes the first night. We now have our proper table places. There are five people at ours, an elderly but extremely pleasant couple of New Zealanders and a young mother returning with her four-year-old boy to her husband in Auckland. The food is particularly pleasant. We have a very good choice at all meals. The portions tend to be small but with four courses at most meals we've nothing to complain about. Our waiter is a bit of a plodder and we're nearly always one of the last tables to be out of the dining room. However, when he's on form he's quite one of the better ones.

A STORM

We ran into a very fierce storm. Several of the crew said that they had never run into such a rough one on this boat. The waves threw a lot of spray right over the decks and it was very difficult to walk. It calmed down yesterday and the sea was almost like a millpond. I think it must have been because we were coming into the Sargasso Sea.

AMUSEMENTS AT SEA

Recently the ship has come alive with entertainment and sports. On Tuesday night we went to the pictures where they showed "The Little Hut", all out on the open deck under an awning. Last night we had what was called a "Book Dinner" in which everyone had to draw a picture, representing the title of a book, on a card and pin it to their coat. After dinner we congregated on the open deck beyond the Verandah Cafe to guess the pictures. Rita drew a corkscrew boy holding a bowl for "Oliver Twist" and I drew a bar, a chest, the letters ER and some towers for "Barchester Towers". Tonight we have a dance. The sports are great fun too. So far we've played Deck Tennis, Bullboard – a kind of darts played with rubber discs on a numbered board, and Peg Quoits. Yesterday the swimming pool was opened and we had a most glorious swim.

We're really getting into the hot weather now. I keep thinking of you all shuddering a bit as the nights draw in and the days get a bit colder. We're coming up to the tropics now.

CABIN INSPECTION

It's most amusing when there is a Captain's Inspection, this happens every other day. Our steward has to bundle us out, in a most polite way. He really has a go at the room, cleaning, polishing, arranging all our toilet kit and ornaments to show them off to the best advantage. Even the bedspreads are put on, and Marcus's toys neatly arranged.

MARCUS

Your grandson is handling the heat very well. He has to be strapped in his pram now, as otherwise he can pull himself onto his knees and look over the side. We had a great day with him yesterday when he said "Ma Ma" for the first time!

CURACAO (KYUOR-RUH-SAU)
We've really run into hot weather now, with temperatures of between 83°C and 89°C, so you can imagine we are making good use of the swimming pool, having often bathed before breakfast.

This morning we had a lot of excitement as we passed many seemingly uninhabited islands. We could see them quite clearly through binoculars and they seemed to consist of dry looking faded grass, rocks, mountains and tall treelike cacti.

We reached Curacao and anchored in the bay where there is an enormous Shell oil refinery. The island seemed to be dotted with huge oil tanks. After a short wait the port authorities came aboard and it was announced that we could go ashore. We put Marcus in the nursery and headed out. The sun was beating down so we spent most of our time in and out of air-conditioned shops, not buying much as everything was dreadfully expensive and we wanted to save our dollars for Panama. In spite of the heat we were absolutely thrilled with everything, jigging along like a couple of school children.

A SUNDAY SCHOOL ON THE SHIP
Recently some mothers mentioned to Rita about a Sunday School on board so yesterday we asked the Purser about it. He seemed to think it a good idea, put up a notice and we had between 16-20 children there in the afternoon out of a total of 36. Rita led the whole service and did it very well despite many adults on the deck listening in. I played the hymns. Everyone, especially the children, seems to think it a great success.

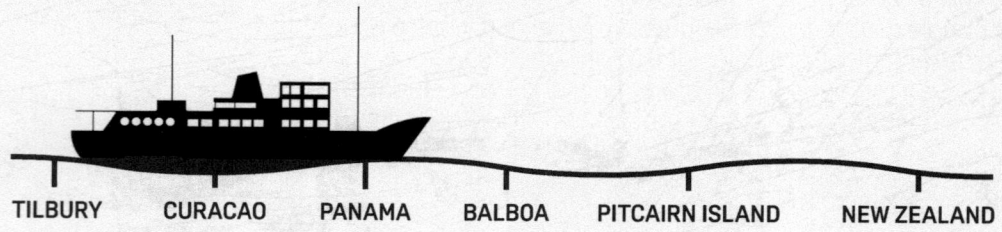

PANAMA CANAL

We arrived at the entrance to the Panama Canal early in the morning. We first passed through three locks after travelling a short way up a narrow culvert surrounded by real tropical vegetation. We suddenly noticed a swarm of moths around us – black with emerald green stripes down their wings. They followed us all the way down the canal, every now and again fluttering on board. After these first three locks, taking us up about 80 feet, we came to a lake where we had to wait two hours while a tanker passed. Apparently the order of ships through the canal is Royal Navy, tankers, then us. We then entered a narrow culvert with steep cliffs on either side covered with trees and shrubs. We came to another three locks which took us down 80 feet to the Pacific Ocean. A huge swing bridge had to open for us at the end of the third lock and then we were heading for Balboa.

BALBOA

We took a taxi into the town and the driver was very good, showing us all the sights on the way. Most of the shops were closing but we managed to buy a few things and spent the rest of the time around the Indian quarter. The next morning we went ashore again and did some shopping and sightseeing before the ship took sail. This was our last journey ashore until Wellington.

FANCY DRESS DANCE

We had a fancy dress parade, Rita dressed in a sheet and carried a gin bottle (Bottled Spirit) and I dressed as a knight with a helmet having no mouthpiece (Silent Night). It was great fun, there must have been nearly a hundred costumes. Apart from films the other entertainment varies between horse-racing, tombola or whist drives. Oh and of course we've had deck games and competitions – all great fun even though we both got knocked out of everything in the first round.

COLD AND ROUGH

Today is very cold, I keep imagining it's like February in England. It's also very rough today. Yesterday we were rolling from side to side and today we're pitching. This makes walking a bit tricky, one moment you're going uphill and the next running downhill. For the last two days a couple of albatrosses have been following us, it's amazing the way they keep up with the ship in the teeth of a very strong wind.

PITCAIRN ISLAND

We had great fun the other day at Pitcairn Island. We arrived off the island at 5pm in a very rough sea, to be met by three long-boats – one a motor boat towing the other two. All the islanders, wearing rough shirts and shorts or oilskins, and with bare feet, were soaking from the waist downward. They brought a small variety of basket work and a lot of fruit, which they sold fast and furiously. We bought one or two odds and ends for Christmas presents and some fruit, including paw-paws. These were a bit like melon to taste but smelt strongly of rancid butter, and we weren't keen on them! The islanders stayed until 7pm and then clambered over the side into their bobbing, dancing, boats. Then they sang us a hymn in beautiful harmonies. It sounded lovely across the darkened water.

> *The last we saw of them were the three lights on their boats hidden one moment by the waves and shining brightly the next.*

APPROACHING NEW ZEALAND

Everyone is getting excited now that we have so few days left before reaching Wellington. I can't say I'm awfully thrilled to be getting off because I suspect the 14 days or so in New Zealand are going to be a little unsettling, especially as we will have a 15-hour train journey from Wellington to Auckland with no dining car! Apparently everyone makes a dive for the refreshment rooms at the few stations where we stop.

TILBURY   CURACAO   PANAMA   BALBOA   PITCAIRN ISLAND   NEW ZEALAND

LETTERS FROM OCTOBER 1958 – NEW ZEALAND

WELCOME AT WELLINGTON
Here we are in New Zealand at last. We came steaming into the harbour safely and saw the lights of the city all around us. It was quite exciting for all who were coming home but for us it meant leaving our last contact with England. The post brought us seven letters! One told us that we will not be sailing for the Islands until November. We were a bit disappointed, as we had wanted to get up there as soon as we could.

WELLINGTON PROGRAMME
They have arranged so much for us here that it will be nice to have a rest in Auckland. Tonight we're going to the Pacific Islanders Church to see films of the Islands; I've been asked next Sunday to give an address at the morning service, to take the whole evening service and to go to a supper afterwards arranged in our honour. On Sunday Rita has to go to meet the women of one of the local churches.

Last night we met Rev. Bob Challis who is in charge of all the Islands Church work in N.Z. and has been a missionary in the Cooks. He was very pleasant and easy to talk to but put us right on a number of things.

SIGHTSEEING AND MEETING PEOPLE
The weather here so far has been glorious spring weather. We've been out a lot already in the wonderful sunshine, up to the park, down to the sea at Lyall Bay, and around the city of Wellington. This afternoon we went along to the House of Representatives and watched Parliament in session.

I was shown around the Boys' Brigade headquarters here, then I went to meet a Mr. McEwan, the Commissioner for Island Territories, a useful Government contact.

OCTOBER PLANS

At last we have some definite plans. We leave Wellington for Auckland on 11th October and sail from there somewhere between 17th – 20th October. We're staying here for two days of the Annual Assembly of the Congregational Union and at the Welcome Meeting and Tea we have to sit at the top table!

AN ISLAND CHURCH DANCE

We went down to a social dance at the Islands Church on Thursday, which was great fun. They mostly danced rock'n'roll but they did perform a traditional Cook Island drum dance.

LUNCH AND SUPPER AT CHURCH

On Sunday we went to the church service. The church was absolutely packed full. Forty Auckland boys were there and we stayed for a lunch given in their honour. The tables were loaded with big bowls of chicken, chop-suey, salads, potatoes and rice, all of which were eaten with fingers, though we were allowed knives and forks. The evening service was quite full too, and it was followed by a supper in our honour. The Sunday School put on a little concert and a quintet sang a sacred song. We had tea and cakes, as well as speeches.

MARCUS

On Monday we moved up here, to Tawa Flat, a district some 8 miles out of Wellington. It's very pleasant here and the people have four children of their own, so Marcus is thoroughly enjoying himself. Marcus has started crawling properly and moves at a terrific pace. He is getting very cheeky – has taken to blowing his food out and is highly amused if he can score a direct hit. All of which makes it difficult to keep a straight face.

SUNDAY SCHOOL ANNIVERSARY

On Sunday I went to the Pacific Islanders' Congregational Church Sunday School Anniversary. They had hired the Concert Chamber at the Town Hall, which must have held a good thousand. It was jammed full with Islanders, including several standing at the back.

LETTERS FROM NOVEMBER 1958 — FINALLY ARRIVED

ARRIVAL AT RAROTONGA

At last we're here! And I notice from the date that it's almost exactly two months to the day. How nice it is to be really settled, at least for a bit, and in a house of our own even for a few months. We're just revelling in this suddenly new-found freedom from living with others.

We were swung off the Maui in a sort of chair-basket and landed in some huge kind of rowing boat – holding, I suppose, some fifty people when fully loaded – and towed to shore by a tug.

WONDERFUL WELCOME

Our welcome here was wonderful. Bernard Thorogood came and met us on board and helped with luggage and so on; and while still on the ship we were presented with our first garland of very strongly scented, highly coloured, flowers. When we arrived at the quay we were met by Janette Thorogood, Glassy Strickland (Secretary of Cook Islands Christian Church) and the local pastor of Avarua Church. Then, still garlanded, we were led between drawn up ranks of Boys' Brigade and Girl Guides. My! Did we feel important! Quite like royalty.

MEETING THE STUDENTS

Bernard drove us to his house beside the training college. At the steps of the house we were met by ranks of the ten students, wives one side, husbands the other, and, in front, a church leader who gave us a traditional Cook Island welcome, shouting and waving a spear. Of course when he brandished the spear Marcus, instead of being duly scared, as we expected, waved back! Rita saw this, and I don't know how she kept a straight face. We were introduced to the students, Rita was given a garland by each wife, so she finished up with seven garlands, Marcus had two little ones and I had four; the last two being given, one by the students and the other by a pastor.

We attended a short service in the college chapel, a delightful building with white-washed walls and blue end curtain, and a cross made of glass inserted into the wall, so the sun shines in through the cross.

INTRODUCTION TO THE HOUSE

Our house stands in a corner of this large compound. We have two bedrooms, a living room, kitchen, bathroom and lavatory, with a wide verandah running along the front and back.

I hope you now have an idea of what we look like in our new surroundings. We're all keeping very fit and have not been bitten once, though we've had to deal with a large flying beetle round the light!

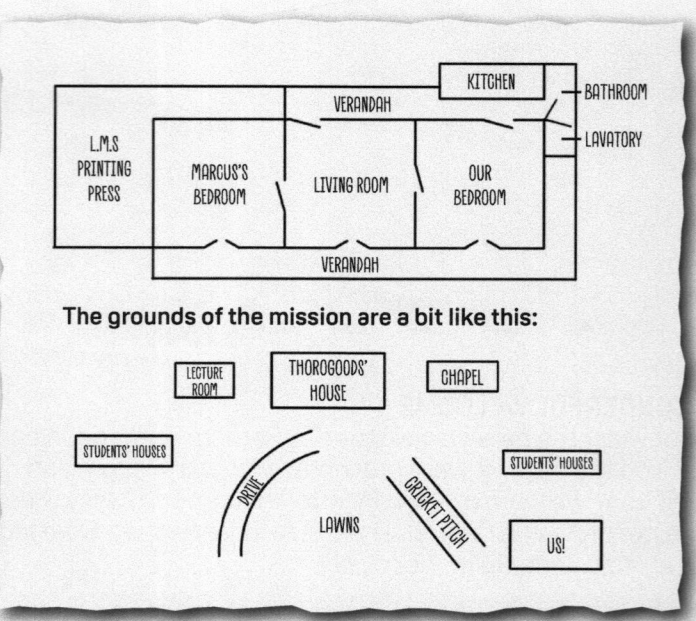

The grounds of the mission are a bit like this:

MARCUS WAKES TOO EARLY

Marcus has not been sleeping well but thankfully he has done better the past two nights, though he still wakes up for good before 5am. Everyone seems to be about and on the move by that time – except the Thorogoods and ourselves! School begins at 7.30am here and ends at 12.30pm.

PREACHING AT NIKAU

We've been to two "welcome feasts" so far, and there are at least five more to come. The first was given by the Rarotongan Council of Churches and the second by the local church at Avarua. Next week we have another at the Nikau Church, where I preached today. We filed into the church and sat in the Missionary's Pew. All the churches have one of these, a bit in the style of the Victorian churches with their pews at the side for the gentry. Then the church filled up with the Boys' Brigade and Girl Guides. The colours were received and the notices given out before the normal service began.

After the sermon I had to stay in the pulpit for the two-minute silence and when the service was over Rita and I had to take the march past and inspection. Then we had tea, sandwiches and cakes, so we didn't get back here until about noon.

PREACHING AT AVARUA CHURCH

Last Sunday I preached the sermon here in Avarua. Of course these sermons have to be simplified so that they can be readily interpreted. For instance there are no Maori words for abstract ideas and if you are not careful all English words will be translated quite literally. So you have to watch your English very carefully which makes you much more grammatically correct in normal conversation.

GARDEN PARTY AT THE RESIDENCY

Last week we had to go to a Garden Party at the Residency in honour of a ministerial party from New Zealand, including the Minister for Island Territories. It was a big "do", with about 300 European and Maori guests. Some Maori dancing was performed by Titikaveka schoolchildren.

FOOD
Last week I went with the Thorogoods to a feast held by Makea Margaret Ariki. It was in honour of the new Legislative Assembly which is being held this month. Rita had to go to the opening of a new clinic, and this was followed by a feast. Fortunately at all these feasts there is a good deal of food which we can eat, chicken, salad, potatoes. Real Maori food includes raw fish in vinegar, kumara, a sweet potato, taro, a gluey potato, and sweetmeats such as banana and pineapple mixed up with arrowroot.

Makea (m-aa-k-ee-aa)
Rarotongan for "Queen", a title for a no longer exercised office.

DRIVE TO THE HOLIDAY HUT
In spite of all this social round we are able to get away now and then. Yesterday we had a picnic at "the Hut". A small Maori-style hut permanently lent to the missionary for a quiet place. It stands right on the beach, with real silver sand down from the tiny back verandah to the deep blue green water, with the huge breakers, sometimes 12 feet or more high, over the coral reef in the background. The hut is terribly primitive. The walls are made of wooden stakes covered with palm leaves. There is a thatched roof, and the floors are of coral cement. The hut is divided into about six tiny rooms and though it is so small, it is an ideal place for a short holiday.

FISHING
We were uninvited spectators of a crowd of Maori fishermen. When they sight a shoal of fish they paddle their outrigger canoes into a complete circle round the fish and drop in a circular net which they draw closer until the fish are trapped. Then they spear them. Those they caught yesterday were like huge trout which took to leaping over the net, clearing the water by anything up to 4 feet. They have to be very careful with these particular fish, for if one hits you in the stomach, it can knock you out. Fortunately we were noticed on the beach by the fisherman and presented with two fish, which we all had for supper.

COCKROACHES, SPIDERS AND ANTS

Our bungalow is a lovely place to live in apart from the animal life, which we are now getting used to. We have lots of large cockroaches scuttling about all over the place. Then there are spiders – Tarantulas – quite harmless and good to have around as they eat the mosquitos, but they are the most fearsome looking creatures. There are also ants – tiny little insects about half the size of those at home but very destructive. You've only got to leave a tiny crumb on the draining board and you have a swarm round in no time. So all the food has to be kept either in our fridge or in food safes with legs standing in tins of water.

INDIAN MYNAH BIRDS

Another nuisance is the Indian Mynah bird. These dart in and out of the kitchen pinching any scrap of food we've left around. They are there even if we've gone out of the kitchen for a couple of minutes. These birds were apparently imported from India many years ago and it seems that they have destroyed all the other bird life. So we have no glorious parrots or anything else like them. Of course we have moths, but these are harmless and don't even eat clothes – the cockroaches do that for us.

Every morning we have to remember to clear up dead bees from the floor. They fly in every night and go round and round the light until they drop exhausted and settle down to die on the floor. We nearly always have to clear up two or three in the morning.

RASTUS THE RAT

The other day we had a great time trying to board up all the rat holes in the kitchen and bathroom. We discovered that our friend "Rastus" the rat was coming in and out of the shower run away in the bathroom which is only a hole in the wall. We thought we'd kept him out successfully until the other evening when I went out into the kitchen to hear a lot of scuffling and to see Rastus race across the floor and out beside the sink run away, which is only a tin pipe in an ill-fitting hold in the wall. This we've blocked and have seen no more of Rastus. I don't know how soon it will be before he finds another hole.

WELCOME FEAST AT NIKAU

Recently we went to our second welcome feast, at Nikau. This was a lovely evening. The Nikau church is quite small in comparison with some others and thus there is much more of a "happy family" atmosphere about the place. We went with Bernard and Janette, and Tarin and Tangi (Cook Island pastor at Wellington and his wife), the six of us sat down at a table on the verandah. Then boys from the local Boys' Brigade began serving the meal, complete with waiters napkins over their arms, which they used to handle every plate of food! We started with soup, then chicken cutlets, with potato salad, kumara, taros (potato), cabbage, arrowroot, pork and still more whole chickens. The meal was completed with jelly and ice cream.

Then began the speeches and the present giving, accompanied by being garlanded with about six "eis" for Rita and myself. The gifts were a mat and a bedspread. Apparently this is the customary Rarotongan gift so by the time we have visited all the churches we'll have six of each!

LANGUAGE STUDY

My language study goes steadily on. I've now learnt a good greeting to give to all the churches we visit.

Kia orawa ki te anoa o te Atua – Greetings and the peace of God be on you

ARORANGI

We both had to go out to a parade and welcome tea from the Boys' Brigade, and Girl Guides of Arorangi. This was a perfect scream as we were given "eis" but not round our necks – these were put on our heads!

Also at Arorangi, we went to a church feast at which we had the usual Island food and, this time, no knives or forks! Still, it was great fun man-handling pork and gravy into one's mouth; fortunately we didn't have jelly or ice cream! We received a lovely bedspread from them, and, instead of the usual mat, we had hats.

UNSEASONABLE WEATHER

The weather here has been a bit unusual and certainly unseasonable. We are now in the hurricane season well and truly, though we've not had a hurricane yet. But these things certainly can mess the weather up quite a bit. There was one rumbling around Fiji the other day but it passed a good many miles west of us. However it caused us to have some very heavy rain and high winds.

We have had pouring rain here for two days, accompanied by a sticky humid atmosphere that makes everything damp. We're told that it can go on for three to four days at a stretch but I should be well out of it tomorrow as Bernard and I are flying to Aitutaki to measure up the bungalow.

MARCUS

Now that Marcus has passed his first birthday he is growing rapidly, mentally and physically. And as soon as we've sung "Amen" he leans forward on Rita's lap to kiss us goodnight. He doesn't always settle straightaway; sometimes he's so full of beans that he races up and down in his cot as if being chased by a greyhound.

He loves to play with the books in the bookcase – unfortunately low enough for him to reach. Knowing that he mustn't touch them, the little monkey makes a bee-line for them as soon as our backs are turned and begins pulling them out and throwing them across the room. When we come back he either sits there and scolds us and starts putting them back; or he bounds across the room, sits down and laughs! It's difficult to be cross, but we persevere.

Happy 1st Birthday Marcus!

LETTERS FROM DECEMBER 1958 – CHRISTMAS TIME IN RAROTONGA

RAROTONGAN WEDDING
We have just been to a wedding. It was between one of the daughters of the Makea Ariki and the Radio Officer of the Maiu Pomare. It was of course a big wedding, with hundreds of guests. We sat at the top table and thoroughly enjoyed ourselves. The meal consisted of chicken, pork, salad, paw-paws, raw fish, taro and kumara, and chop suey, followed by jelly and ice cream, and wedding cake. After the wedding feast came the customary presentation of gifts to the Bride and Groom. This afternoon the couple must have received at least 25 island-made mats and at least as many bedspreads. They also received enough dress material to stock the bride almost for life, together with a lot of money.

SPEECH MAKING
At every welcome I have to make a speech, and as it has to be translated I can't go on for long. In a way that is a good thing, since I try to say something different on each occasion. You begin a speech here with traditional greetings; to all the people, the church pastor, the deacons, the members; to the Sunday School, the Boys' Brigade and Girl Guides and all the young people; to the Arikis, the Rangitiras, the Mataiapos – all hereditary titles; to the members of the Legislative Assembly and the Government. You can guess that all this can take a long or a short time, depending on whether one elaborates it or not.

RAROTONGAN CHURCHES
The churches here are built in the late Victorian style with wooden interiors and cement-coral mixtures outside. The pulpits are central, with a communion table in front, and there are always two side pews on either side, facing the pulpit. Those on the right facing the pulpit are for the missionary and his family and those on the left for the Arikis, etc. All the pulpits seem to be very high and often I can only just see over the top of them, which makes preaching from them a bit difficult. The churches vary quite a lot in their size though most of them would hold at least 500 quite easily and be full for the morning service. They have no choirs as every Cook Islander seems to be born with a gift for harmonising, regardless of whether they know the tune or not.

FLIGHT TO AITUTAKI

The plane to Aitutaki was a very small Dekota, carrying only nine passengers. I was lucky to be sitting on the side nearest the window so I got a good view of the take off and most of the journey. I can't say I'm very impressed with air travel, although it's certainly quick. We had a smooth take off and the landing was good, though a bit bumpy, on account of the airstrip being a bit rough and ready. The journey takes only an hour and a half, compared with 12 hours by sea.

EXPERIENCES AT AITUTAKI

The bungalow is delightful, with an enormous great flamboyant tree in the front garden. This has a beautiful red flower on it and gives a magnificent shade from the sun.

We had a welcome feast and then spent the afternoon touring the three villages on the island in the back of a lorry, waving to everyone and visiting all the churches. In the evening we had a service at the large church in Arutanga, at which I had to preach the sermon. The church building is huge, seating about a thousand, and, being lit for our purposes by petrol pressure lamps, it was quite ghostly.

We turned into bed at about 10pm and I was awakened by Bernard at about 11.30pm, chasing a huge great land crab out of the bedroom! Apparently these are quite common there, coming out at night and making quite a nuisance of themselves by scuttling all over the place and creating an awful noise.

AT NGATANGIIA

The rest of my time since this visit has been spent by me in preaching and by Rita in visiting Women's Institutes. We have also had a welcome feast at Ngatangiia, at which we received, you'll never guess, a bedspread and a mat! Rita had a pretty shell necklace, made of tiny little shells with five big cowries in it.

COMMUNION SERVICES

At every service the pastor stands in the pulpit whilst a deacon sits at the communion table. His job is to announce the hymn numbers. The churches remain quite full for the communion service so you can guess that these sometimes take a long time. At the first one we attended we were puzzled when the cloth covering the table was removed to see trays of what looked like empty cups. It turned out that they were actually full of coconut milk which, of course, is transparent. Drink is prohibited on the Island, so this is their substitute.

CONTROL OF DRINKING

The L.M.S. has quite a strong voice in the Assembly because so many of the members are men brought up in L.M.S. churches. Let me give you an example. I mentioned that alcoholic drinks are prohibited. This is not strictly true, as it can be obtained on a doctor's certificate. This has led to a complete farce as the doctors tend to give out certificates indiscriminately. There was also an idea of setting up a licensed hotel here, which would have firmly set the Maoris in the habit of drinking. The Cook Islands Church set up a petition to the Assembly proposing a complete overhaul of the system of obtaining permits for drinking – not allowing any private person or corporation to have a licensed bar; but allowing the sale of drink to all people, the amount to be issued to be subject to their income and number of dependents. Mr. Thorogood had to appear before a Select Committee to give the reasons for this proposal and he had to begin by telling the members of the Committee that they must not think of him as a missionary but must feel quite free to ask any questions or to disagree with what he said. Otherwise they would have calmly agreed to everything he said simply because he was the "Papaa". The proposal came before the Assembly and, with only one or two minor alterations, was passed unanimously!

Alcohol prohibition in the Cook Islands officially ended in 1975, marking a shift in the nation's social and economic landscape. Prior to this, strict regulations – heavily influenced by missionary values and colonial policies – had restricted the sale and consumption of alcohol. The lifting of prohibition aligned with broader modernisation efforts, allowing for the development of licensed bars, resorts and duty-free outlets, which catered to both locals and international visitors.

TREES AND FRUIT

When we first arrived we were a little disappointed not to find any really bright colours on the trees or in the gardens, but now that we've come into summer we're finding far more glorious colours. There is one particular tree called the "flamboyant" with a brilliant red flower that covers the outspread branches completely, giving the impression of a pillar of fire. There are also lots of "frangipani" trees, from which most of the garlands are made. These are grown in all sorts of colours, the most popular being white with a yellow border though you do see flowers in pink, yellow and peach colours.

In the compound here there are the usual coconut trees, bearing fruit most of the year round, as well as two or three enormous scotch pines, one of which is supposed to have been planted by John Williams back in the 1840s.

Our back garden has two or three orange trees, one grapefruit tree, and a banana tree, with two big bunches. If we get a bit more real summer weather they should ripen quickly and we ought to be getting plenty of fresh fruit.

THE SCENE FROM THE BUNGALOW

At the moment I'm sitting out on the front verandah of our bungalow watching all that's going on in front of me. There are quite a lot of Indian Mynah birds around at this moment, twittering and tweeting. As I said in my letter, they are the only birds we get here and they're a bit of a nuisance. They imitate quite well so there seem to be a number of different birds by their songs. Out in front of me I can see the big field belonging to the compound. Beyond the field I can see a very high hill covered with trees. It looks quite picturesque. Over to the right there's a large flamboyant tree which is just coming out into bloom. The colours on that tree are really glorious.

CHRISTMAS PRESENTS
Christmas was quite hectic. It all began several days beforehand, when we had to wrap up 120 packets of sweets and 70 small presents. These consisted of flannels, soaps, and a comb for ladies; notebooks, pencils and soaps for men. These 70 presents were distributed at the Christmas Eve party for the choir and students. In addition, the students received dresses and dress lengths, shirts, shorts, tobacco, razor blades and a mirror. We all had to run the party with the usual old party games! I think they all enjoyed themselves and we got to bed just before midnight.

A BUSY CHRISTMAS MORNING
On Christmas morning I dashed off at 7.20am for Morning Communion with the English community, which Bernard conducted and at which I had to play the rather wheezy harmonium. After a quick breakfast we got ourselves ready for the next service, a Maori one, at 9.30am. Each of the districts of Avarua, of which there are about five, sang one of their special chants before the service began. Then, with the choir, we went up the road to sing carols and distribute sweet parcels at the hospital. We paraded through all the wards and Bernard and I shook hands with everyone. We had a short service in the main men's ward conducted by Bernard, with a brief sermon by the local pastor. Everyone seemed pleased with the gifts.

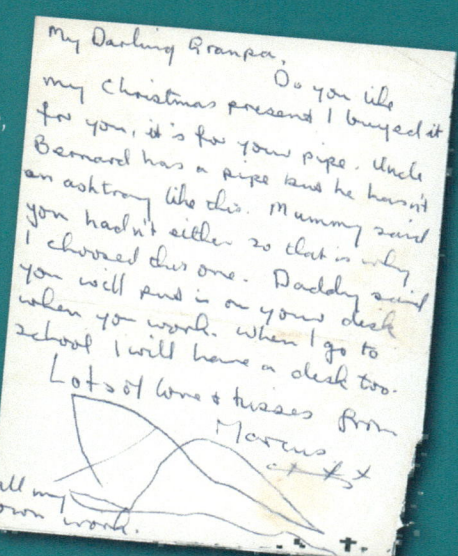

CHRISTMAS AFTERNOON AND EVENING
We went up to the mission house for our Christmas dinner of cold ham and tongue, potato salad, beetroot; and Christmas pudding, jelly, trifle, nuts, raisins, dates, and ginger. We went out again, with the choir, up to the T.B. Sanatorium with more presents. This is a beautiful place set high on a hill overlooking the air strip and beach, with a glorious view. We spent some time there, speaking with all the patients, including a student's wife who has leprosy. Her husband is with her and does great work in the hospital, giving lectures, and taking services – all after only a year at Takamoa! After this we drove off to the prison where we gave out bags of sweets. There were about 15 prisoners to visit. Most of the prisoners were there for petty theft, larceny, and illicit beer distilling.

A DAY AT THE SEASIDE
On Saturday we went out to the shack at Titikaveka and had our first bathe. You have to be careful to wear shoes here, as you could get a nasty cut from the coral, strewn all over the sea.

MARCUS
Marcus swam with us and is taking to the sea like a fish! He spent most of the afternoon flinging handfuls of sand in all directions, clambering in and out of holes which he dug, and falling flat on his face, coming up for air like some kind of snowman gone wrong, with two bright eyes peering through piles of sand.

A DAYS WORK PART 1 – IN THE STUDY
Today I started working on the verandah trying to get a syllabus out for the Boys' Brigade Bible Class next year. So next year we're doing the Prophets, twelve lessons in all.

This work was interrupted by one of the students bringing over the mail which Bernard had been down to the Post Office to collect. No letter-boxes here, we just have a box at the Post Office.

A DAYS WORK PART 2 – FIXING AN AERIAL
Then I decided to try and get a longer aerial fixed for our wireless, so I got one of the students to climb a coconut tree and fasten the end of my 100 ft. wire to the top. He sat up there, 70 feet up, quite happily for some long time but eventually got it fixed.

A DAYS WORK PART 3 – EVENING PRAYERS
I got back to Boys' Brigade Bible Classes and this took me up to Evening Prayers to which all students go, and which we all take in turn, my turn, of course, being as yet in English. However, I have written with my own fair hand a speech in Maori which I'm to give at the six village districts of Avarua on New Year's Eve. I've got to get Bernard to go over it tomorrow in case I find I'm telling them how to pull the teeth out of a chicken when I think I'm saying "A Happy New Year".

Kia Orana – May you live long, and may you live well!

SMASHED WINDOWS

They'd had fun at the house this afternoon. The student who climbed my tree was supposed to be cutting the lawn in the front of the house, which he did; and whilst moving away somehow churned up a small stone which went flying through a window. Apparently Bernard and Janette thought they were being shot at! However, all is now mended – with sellotape.

MARCUS

He's getting on well with his first walking attempts now. He can manage about ten steps, sometimes all at once, and sometimes with a break in the middle; when he stops, sways perilously, regains his balance and totters on. He loves it when Rita and I stand a yard or two apart and he walks from one to the other. As soon as you hold out your hands to him he starts to race towards you, shrieking with delight, sometimes with such excitement that he falls down with a plop half way across.

However, he still likes to be able to crawl. He's taken now to standing on his legs, bending his body until his head touches the ground and looking through his legs; the world must seem so peculiar all tops-turvy. Of course it's all the funnier if you also get down and look at him through his legs; he laughs so much that he nearly always collapses.

LETTERS FROM JANUARY 1959 – THE FLOOD

GETTING HOT
It's getting very hot here now and bringing out the mosquitos who don't seem to be able to read the advice on insect repellent creams, so we are having quite a few bites between us. Even now, at 9.30pm, it's 75°C so you can imagine that every door and window is open all night long.

TORRENTIAL RAIN
The big news in this letter is our recent torrential downpour. It started last Monday with a light fall of rain which got steadily worse all day. We went out in the evening to dinner with the Resident Commissioner. We borrowed the car and on the way back drove along some roads flooded to a depth of two inches. It poured in torrents all night long making a dreadful noise on our corrugated iron roof, and in the morning a good deal of the field between us and the Mission House was well under water.

FLOODING
Where the land lays in a valley between the road and the mountains had become completely under water up to five feet with children using the flooded areas as bathing pools, swimming about in all their clothes. Many houses were badly flooded too.

We came to a place where the water was swirling across the road and the car stopped right in the middle. Tariu, who was also with us, and I jumped out to push us to dry land and landed in water up to our knees, how it didn't come into the car I don't know. Within a minute a crowd of people who had been trying to salvage their homes came across to help us! Such is the character of the people, even in the midst of all their own troubles they could come across and help us without even being asked.

On the way home we discovered that the private road leading to our compound was under water, the school fields next to the compound were like a brown sea, again being used as a swimming pool, being waist deep.

DROWNING AT AVARUA
Rita and I went out in the afternoon to survey it all, wearing sandals, shorts and macs and had great fun wading through it all. We discovered later that the other side of Avarua was worse than this, for in places the water was nine-feet deep; so deep, in fact, that a boy was drowned. The rain stopped on Wednesday morning and we found that in 36 hours we had had 11 inches of rain, a record stretching as far back as 1936, when they had 11 inches in 24 hours.

A LINK WITH 1860
I wonder sometimes how the early missionaries managed, with news from their families only once every year or two. What a lot we have to be thankful for! Today I was taken right back to the early missionary days and was made to realise how short a time the modern missionary movement has been going, particularly in the South Seas. We went to a rather belated Welcome Feast at Titikaveka and there met an old chap who we reckoned must be at least 90. He said he thought he was baptised by the Rev. Crouch, who was here in the 1860s!

ANOTHER WELCOME FEAST
This feast at Titikaveka was one that had been postponed because of the flood in which we got stuck a week or two ago. We didn't think they would invite us again because there's such a lot of expense and preparation put into them. But they turned up trumps by giving us a very good Feast today. We nearly didn't get to this one either! Half way there we came upon a tree that had been blown down and completely blocked the road. Fortunately we found we were able to drive round it through someone's land.

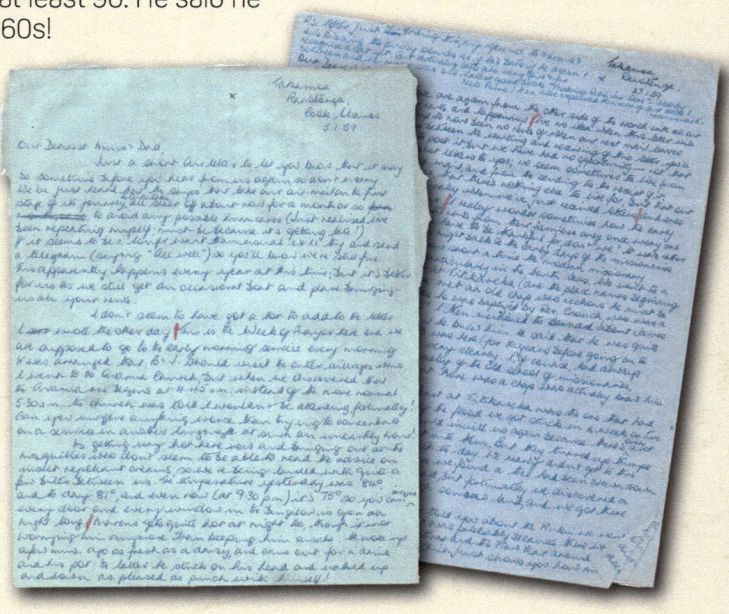

A PAGEANT

At the beginning of this month we went to a "Nuku" The word means "army" or "company" and in this case signifies a pageant which a large company of the people come to see. It takes place only in Rarotonga and only once in two years, so we were quite lucky to see it.

We saw some thrilling, some well-acted, and some rather comic performances from the Sunday schools. They were:

- David and Abigail (I must admit that we all had to look that one up before we went).
- David and Goliath.
- Isaiah and Sennacherib, in which the parts of Hezekiah and Sennacherib were played by children dressed in the most glorious sparkling robes. It also included the very realistic and solemn slaughter of the Assyrian forces by a little girl dressed as an angel, who waved a silver sword over the army while they slept. Unfortunately the Rarotongans have a terrific sense of humour so that even this solemn moment was enlivened when soldiers came in the morning to look at the dead troops and lifted up arms and legs, only to find that these remained in the air!
- John the Baptist, with a wonderful and clever dance by Salome with her traditional seven veils. These were all neatly tucked into the belt of her dress and thrown away one by one. We also saw the Baptist beheaded, made more realistic by the body having a cloak thrown over it and convulsing up and down just after his head had been cut off! Most gruesome.
- Elijah, being fed by the ravens and restoring the widow's son.
- Ruth and Naomi. This again was well performed and quite moving.

At the beginning and end of it all we were treated to a real feast of modern music! All the six groups had a different marching song which they all sang while parading together. To listen to six quite different songs being sung at the tops of their voices is quite an experience, especially when most groups were accompanied at least by guitars and drums, while some even had cornets.

THE BRIGADE AND GUIDE CAMPS

We have just finished our Girl Guide and Boys' Brigade Camps which were held at Nikau for ten days. We went, of course, to the opening ceremony, Rita to the Guides and I to the Boys' Brigade.

On the Sunday we had parade services and a march past at Nikau Church in the morning and at Napou in the evening, which includes answering set Bible questions and a lot of singing mingled with hula dancing with even the old people swinging and swaying their hips about.

On Wednesday they had a Tere (pronounced Terry) party which is a kind of picnic. They piled into about five trucks, drove to the outskirts of each village and marched through with their brass band. This draws a crowd of people to the roadside – and they make gifts of money. Every time this happens the parade has to stop while an officer calls out in a loud voice how much the person has given and everyone gives three cheers. This can be embarrassing if you give anything less than two shillings. It took them the best part of the day to get round the villages and they were all very tired by the end of it.

On the Friday afternoon the boys held their march-past and display and in the evening performed more items, mostly singing. The following afternoon there was the same inspection and march-past by the girls and a proper campfire in the evening.

Parade services and a Uapou were again held on Sunday and on Monday morning we went to their farewell service in the church. There were many tears, the Islanders being very emotional.

MARCUS

A TENNIS PARTY
The Titikaveka feast today was followed by a Tennis Party at the house of the Scout Commissioner to the Cooks. He is at present in New Zealand and we were entertained by his Maori wife. After a few enjoyable games we were beaten by the rain. We decided that next time we go there we must get a babysitter for Marcus, the house not being one for little boys. If he wasn't running over the court, he was chasing chickens; if he wasn't throwing sand in some lovely tropical violet plants, he was trying to throw himself in the pond; and if he wasn't trying to let the budgerigars loose from their cage, he was letting himself loose on everybody and everything with a tennis racquet!

FEEDING THE CHICKENS
When Marcus saw Janette going out to feed the chickens he shouted to her until she noticed him. He loves chickens. We often have hosts of them coming to our back door for bread which they seem to know Rita will give them. Marcus squeals with delight and makes very good imitation cockerel noises at them. They've recently taken to wandering into the kitchen and then Marcus spends all his time in unsuccessful attempts to catch them.

A COW IN THE GARDEN
We had a cow in the front garden for a few days recently to clear out an old vegetable patch. Sometimes, however, they wander in, quite uninvited if we happen to leave the front gate open and then some students rush down and the cow is ignominiously chased out. However, as soon as Marcus saw this, he got very excited and when the cow started moo-ing or grunting or whatever it is that cows do to converse with other cows — it was no time before he could moo or grunt as well as the best cow in the Cook Islands.

COCKROACHES NO LONGER TERRORISE
Can you imagine having a huge bunch of bananas hanging up in your kitchen? That's what we've got now. The best thing to do with bananas is to pick them green and hang them up indoors to ripen. There must be at least fifty on this half-bunch! It's now 8.50pm, with a light fall of rain. The moths are beginning to fly, the cockroaches to crawl and the rats to scuttle but what do we care for such small fry any longer!

LETTERS FROM FEBRUARY 1959 – GOING BANANAS

BANANAS GALORE
People have been wonderfully kind and not a day goes by without some sort of gift. We have had about four bunches of bananas and the smallest bunch has 50 on it – the largest nearly 90. One morning we had a lobster brought in, still alive!

STUDENTS' WIVES MIND MARCUS
As we're living in the Training College we've always one out of half-a-dozen students' wives to ask to look after Marcus. One of the wives is on duty in the kitchen at the house for a month at a time and often Rita will ask her to look after Marcus. She also comes over to our bungalow in the morning to wash up and make the beds. Of course, Marcus has his favourites amongst them being Tapua, Tutai (Tootaee) and Nui (Nooee) and they're always only too pleased to have him for an hour or two.

SIMPLE LIFE IN THE SHACK
We've just returned from a glorious fortnight in the shack. On the whole we had pretty good weather, the second week being better than the first, and we were able to swim twice a day most days. From our back verandah it was a matter of six steps to the sand and from there about twelve to the sea. Of course it was a bit primitive. There was no electricity and every night we had to light the lamps. Sometimes the water pressure would give out and the emergency tank, holding 40 gallons of water, would run dry at the same time, making us walk 300 yards along the beach to a tap and carry back a couple of buckets full in drenching rain. And, of course, there were crabs. There were crab holes all round the shack but only one came inside. He was about six inches in diameter, the biggest I'd seen.

HOW BANANAS RIPEN
I'll tell you how bananas ripen. We had to hang the branch of banana bunches from a beam and slowly but surely they began to turn, starting with the lowest ones, from their natural green to the better known yellow. That's all there is to it except that you must remember to cover the branch with a sack when there are Mynah birds about.

HOLIDAY WEATHER

We have just finished a fortnight's holiday round the other side of the island. We were living in a typical Maori house with bamboo walls and a thatched roof. No electricity and a temperamental water tap! The first week was terribly windy and it rained most days, which kept us in a great deal, but the last week was so hot at times that we lived either in the water or on the beach. Practically the whole of this house went with us so we had to hire a truck to get the stuff out and back. It was a proper case of "moving home"!

We will only be in this smaller mission house for another week; then we move over to the main house ready to carry on Mr. and Mrs. Thorogood's work. Ta Pere arrives on the same boat the Thorogoods leave on. Ta and his wife will be living in this house so the change over will be a bit of a rush.

This should be a fairly quiet week for us, which is all to the good as it will be a hectic time for the Thorogoods and we will probably be able to help them a good deal.

The Main Mission House

LETTERS FROM MARCH 1959 – MOVING HOUSE

AFTER THE THOROGOODS' DEPARTURE
We have now moved into the Mission House and kept busy all day long. To give you some idea, here is a rough weekly time table, alongside which there is tons of office work to complete:-

MONDAY	TUESDAY	WEDNESDAY	THURSDAY	FRIDAY
LECTURE PREPARATION ODD JOBS PASTORS' MEETING B.B. OFFIERS' MEETING	NEW TESTAMENT LECTURES STUDENTS GAMES NIGHT	LECTURE NOTES ODD JOBS	NEW TESTAMENT LECTURES SERMON CLASS	OLD TESTAMENT LECTURES ENGLISH CHOIR PRACTICE

HELP FOR NIUE
I wish you could see Rita at this moment. She's been sorting out all sorts of boxes, trying to find some clothing to send to Niue Island, which has just had a dreadful hurricane. There are thousands of pounds' worth of damage, including about £80,000 damage to L.M.S. property. We felt nothing of it at all here, in spite of being comparatively close.

MARCUS
Marcus is very well and thoroughly enjoying life; so much so that we had to make some gates for the top and bottom of the stairs as soon as we arrived here. He goes charging off up the stairs at the slightest excuse without any apparent fear at all. He loves this big house, probably because there's so much mischief here that he can get into. There is a lovely big verandah upstairs where he can play happily, except that he has thrown all his toys over the edge onto the heads of unsuspecting people down below.

THE MISSION HOUSE
You asked about this house and here is a rough plan of it:

DOWNSTAIRS
A - Study
B - Desk
C - Workshop
D - Lounge
E - Hall
F - Dining Room
G - Passage
H - Bathroom
J - Kitchen
K - Back Verandah
L - Front Verandah

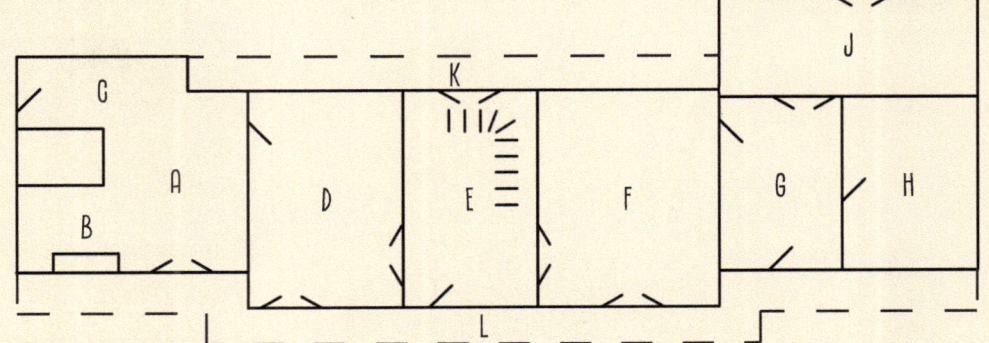

UPSTAIRS
A - Our Bedroom
B - Sitting Room
C - Marcus's Bedroom
D - Landing
E - Stairs
F - Bed
G - Wash Basin (running cold water!)
H - Dressing Table
J - Marcus's Cot
K - Bookcase
L - Chairs
M - Table with wireless and gramophone

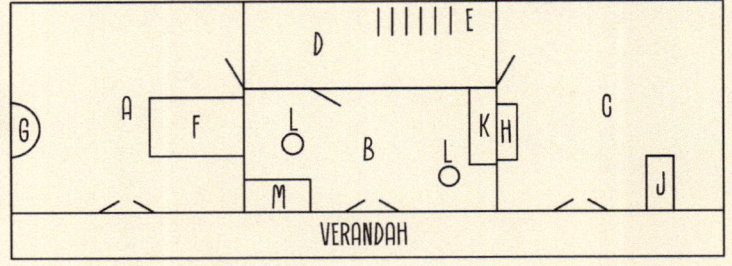

Of course we much prefer it to the old bungalow — no rats here, and it is much fresher as we are on a high piece of ground overlooking the whole compound and can see at a glance what is going on in any corner.

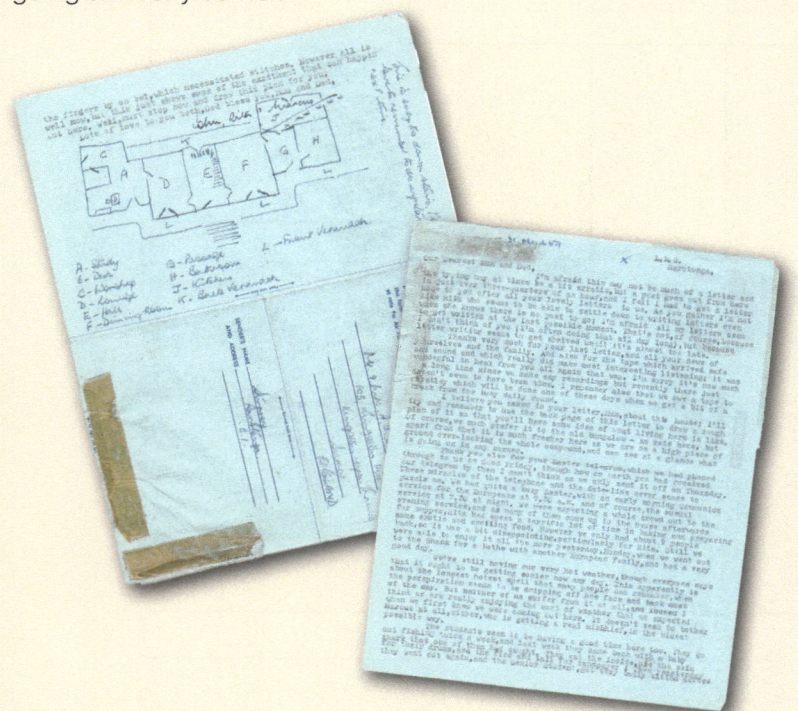

The Main Mission House 1959

Former Mission House 2023

LETTERS FROM APRIL 1959 – IT'S A BUSY LIFE

BUSY RITA

Life is proving very busy at present, but very enjoyable. Rita has her hands full not only with Marcus, who is getting to be a really cheeky, mischievous boy, in the nicest possible way, of course, but also with the students' wives, whom she has to look after, not only with all their occasional aches and pains, but with all the work that they are supposed to be doing. She has a weekly inspection of their houses which takes quite a bit of time, and a good deal of the rest of the week is spent in chivvying them up to make sure their houses look nice for the next inspection. She has also organised a nursery here for the nine children in the compound, which is looked after by two wives each day, all of them taking a turn. And she also has a weekly lecture to give them on a hundred and one different subjects, mostly connected with child welfare.

EVERY DAY A FULL DAY

I have quite a full day every day as well, with lectures to the students three mornings a week, to which also come the six Pastors from the churches on Rarotonga. Two other days a week the students spend fishing, sounds strange, but it does help to supplement their food, while I prowl round the Compound seeing all the jobs which need to be done, writing up lecture notes, interviewing anybody who happens to come in, either for a chat, or for something more serious, and trying to keep the cash books straight, a most ghastly job! Then we both have a Bible Class to take on Sunday afternoon, and a class in the only Senior School in the Group on Monday mornings, on Religious Knowledge. So you see there's not much time for lazing on the tropical beaches under the waving palm trees.

Of course we get some excitement in the College occasionally. Last week the students on a fishing expedition came home with a baby shark, only about two months old, about two feet in length, caught with a spear gun which most of the students use in preference to a line and bait. Sharks are quite valuable as there is a good bit of flesh on them and the skin is used for tightening over their drums, and the fin and tail are used for sandpaper!

THE MAORIS LIKE DRUMS
You'll notice that I mentioned drums. These you can hear being played for a good part of the day. They actually use them a good deal for announcing the picture shows. A truck goes careering off round the Island with about fifteen or twenty boys in the back beating their drums as loudly as they can, and distributing handbills giving details of the pictures to be shown that day. They also use them a lot when the Islanders go round the Island on a picnic.

NO PICNIC SPOTS
They've no nice special picnic spots here so when they go on a picnic they drive right round the Island, stopping in most of the villages on the way, all wearing their brightly coloured "ei" round their heads and necks. It seems so strange to us that on such a delightful sounding island there should be no real beauty spots. Only a strip about half a mile wide all round the island is inhabited and cultivated, and the rest consists of towering mountains and dense scrub. You can climb the mountains, of course, if you feel energetic enough – we've not got that far yet!

PLAGUED BY COCKROACHES
We seem to be plagued at the moment by these wretched flying cockroaches which come zooming into a room and flutter round in absolute panic. When one comes in, we flutter round in absolute panic too, and I often wonder if we don't make each other more frightened. Marcus is the only one who doesn't seem to mind them, and we're only waiting now for the day when he starts trying to catch one.

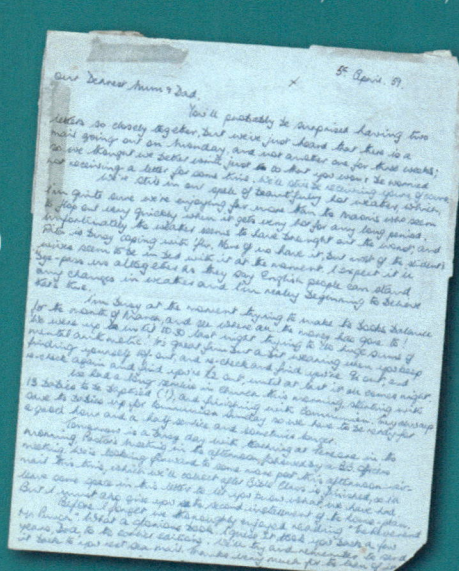

A LONG SERVICE
We had a long service in church this morning, starting with 13 babies to be baptised and finishing with Communion. They always save the babies for Communion Sunday so we have to be prepared for a good hour and a half service, and perhaps longer.

CALLING THE DOCTOR
When a Maori wants the Doctor to call he has to hang a white flag outside his gate so that the Doctor knows, when he rides round the Island. Flags range from a grubby handkerchief to a lady's slip! When you drive round the one Island road you can always see the flags here and there, and even in places where you had no idea that there was a house at all.

PRIMITIVE ROAD-MAKING
We've nothing like tar sealing on our roads. They seem to be made up of earth, flints and stones. We've nothing so grand as road-rollers either — just a grader which is used to spread the rubble evenly when it is put down — about once every six weeks. Then the poor motorists have to use their cars as road-rollers so it's not surprising that the garages' most popular job is puncture mending. I had three in ten days recently.

In dry hot weather every car is followed by a dust storm! So much so that shop and house owners take to watering the roads in front of their premises with hoses. In the wet weather the roads are a sea of mud and every car and truck makes deep ruts all over the place.

LOVELY DRIVES
In spite of this it's often really delightful to go out for a drive round the Island. Some parts remind us often of some of the Surrey lanes with greenery on either side of the road and sometimes with trees meeting overhead to form a dark tunnel. The road is never more than 300 yards from the sea, so we always have the sound of the breakers on the reef.

PICKING COFFEE BEANS
The wives all went out this afternoon into the hills behind the house here on a coffee-picking expedition! They came back with baskets full of coffee beans picked straight off the trees which are growing wild. Apparently you have to soak the beans in water and peel off the outer shell. Then the bean is well-dried and ground and so, hey presto, coffee at your service from your backdoor! Good, isn't it?

RITA MAKING JAM
A short while ago Rita was very busy making 13 pounds of jam out of a fruit which is a cross between a grape and a gooseberry. I can't think what it is called but it tastes good and is a pleasant change from shop bought jams.

MARCUS

At the moment Marcus's one aim in life is to get out of our garden and into the field where he can romp around with Mac the dog. Our one aim is to keep him inside as we get some heavy traffic through Takamoa. We thought we had succeeded until we caught him flat on his tummy sliding underneath one of the gates!

He's now sitting on the top verandah shouting like a barrow boy at the Pastors below who have come for a Church Council meeting. When we were shopping in the village a couple of days ago a drum started beating. The local children at once began to wriggle their hips in time to the music, but Marcus started to march up and down shouting "left-right", connecting the drum with Boys' Brigade Parade.

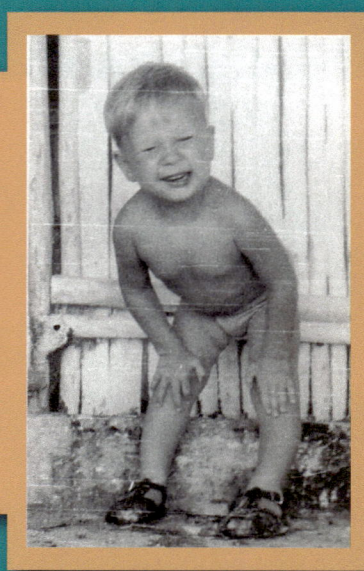

HULA DANCING
I doubt very much whether we will ever learn to hula dance properly because the rhythm which is peculiar to it has to be learnt in childhood. True hula dancing is not which we see in films. That is a good imitation, but definitely not the real thing. The men don't do so much hip swinging as leg and arm shaking. Their limbs look like pieces of elongated rubber attached to a string. It is a most fascinating sight, always hypnotising us. If only we could learn!

LETTERS FROM MAY 1959 – THE BABY EMERGENCY

MARCUS

Marcus is growing very quickly now. He feeds himself very well though sometimes we feel like dressing up in full-length house-coats for meals, with the amount of food that is deliberately aimed at us! We've just found him one of Rita's old school drums to play with now and he marches all over the place bashing at the drum with anything he can lay hands on, shouting "left, right, left, right" etc. We'll have to get him into the Boys' Brigade as soon as we can! We bought him his own, miniature wicker chair today.

MORE STUDENTS ARRIVE

Two more new students and their wives arrived at the College last Sunday. They're from Rakahanga, in the Northern Group. I don't think I've ever told you all the students' names so I'll give you a list, starting with the Senior, and working down. I'll put in the pronunciation of the more difficult ones; the rest should be pronounced as spelt, saying each vowel separately.

- Toka and Tupuna
- Tei (Tay) and Tutai
- Nootai (both o's pronounced) and Rose
- Mangara and Nui
- Tekeu (Teku) and Tepua
- Teariki and Marea (Marie)
- Vaka and Manaha
- Singapu and Eva
- Tihau (Tihow) and Ngaari
- Tianeva (Chianewa) and Mareta

THE BABY THAT STOPPED BREATHING!

We're still finding the work enjoyable as well as strenuous. There is always something to be done. Like this evening, when we suddenly had five husbands and one wife come running panic-stricken up to the house here for "Mama", with a baby who, it seemed, had stopped breathing! Rita took the baby, gave it a hard smack, and all was well again. Mama worked a miracle for them tonight with some quick thinking and a knowledge of children, and everyone is happy again.

AT THE MOVIES

I don't think I've told you about going to the movies here. Of course it's not done for the missionary to go to the ordinary picture show with everyone else. So we have our own show every two or three weeks, depending on what the film is. A member of one of the churches has made his own projector, on which he can show any type of film – from the old silent to cinemascope. He services the projectors at one of the local theatres and so can borrow a film at any time. And if it's worth seeing, he invites us up. On occasions we have to sit through a raving musical, for his tastes and ours don't always agree, but at least it's an evening's relaxation. He's an extremely clever mechanic and has even made himself a searchlight with a terrifically powerful beam.

ISLAND FOODS AND FISH

Prices are quite high here but we are maintaining a modest standard of comfort. In some ways we do very well as occasionally someone brings us fruit or vegetables. The students go fishing twice a week and have to supply the house with fish, which sometimes turns out to be lobster. The other day we had our first taste of Island-grown coffee, prepared by Rita and the wives. It was delicious.

MARCUS

The other day when it poured with rain he went to the front gate and wanted to go out. So I got my umbrella and carried him out to the car, which we drove together into the garage. Then we walked back to the house through the pouring rain. But he wasn't satisfied. Once back inside he pointed outside with one hand and to the umbrella with the other, and said his usual "Ta". So Rita found his wellington boots, gave him an old umbrella, and he went plodding out of the back door, down the side of the house, and out onto the field. He couldn't see exactly where he was going because he kept the umbrella well down over his head, and every now and again he had to stop and lift up the umbrella to get his bearings. Then he plodded on again till he gained the shelter of one of the students' houses, where he remained as happy as anything.

We've found him his own Boys' Brigade cap now, an old unwanted one of very small size which fits his head perfectly. On the Parade day he can strut up and down, wearing his hat and banging away at his tin drum.

LETTERS FROM JULY 1959 — THE AITUTAKI VISIT

OFF TO AITUTAKI
Yes, this is really written on my birthday and I'm having a very Happy Birthday. For some time now we've been trying to get over to Aitutaki to have a look at our bungalow there. We made some enquiries and discovered that a ship is going over there and returning straight away, leaving tomorrow! So we are frantically getting things ready. There's no guarantee that it'll be a smooth crossing as we're having some very rough weather at the moment.

I'm also trying to get on a trip up to Manihiki in the Northern Group — it's about 650 miles distant. This trip won't be for pleasure; I have to try to sort out some trouble in the church there. As yet I can't find a ship to take me, so I don't know when that one will come off.

WE LIKE AITUTAKI
Aitutaki is a wonderful place. At least it seems so on a brief visit, though I don't know what our thoughts may be when we go to live there with no running water, no electricity, no cars and no dogs. But I think that in spite of the lack of all these things it's a much lovelier island than this one. This one is a bit too sophisticated in a rather brash European way. But Aitutaki has a very small European population, able to do far less damage than they've done here. It's quieter too, and less spoilt, which I think means a lot. The house, of course, is wonderful. It's in a pretty good state of repair too, though we will no doubt want to make a few alterations when we get there; not structurally, of course.

COOK ISLANDS CHURCH JOINS NATIONAL COUNCIL
We have had some very good news that the National Council of Churches of New Zealand has accepted the application of the Cook Islands Christian Church to become a member. Bernard had been working for this for some time and he'll be very pleased. For some time the New Zealand Congregational Churches have tried to dissuade us from joining separately from them. They thought we ought to affiliate with them and be represented by them on the Council. We suspected that they wanted this so that they could increase their numeral statistics with our 13,000 members.

RENOVATING STUDENTS' HOUSES
So we are very pleased especially as when a new church joins they give a little present of money. We receive £400, which is going to be spent in renovating the students' houses – Bernard's brilliant suggestion. We knew about the gift coming, though not the amount, so Bernard had suggested that I go ahead and start building some new verandahs on the front of the houses. We've done those for two houses so far but I had refused to do any more until we had some definite promise of the money. The verandahs for one pair of houses cost about £50 so you can understand my hesitation. £50 may not sound a lot of money but to this college it's the earth. However, now we'll be able to go ahead again. Fortunately all the work is done by the students so we have no labour costs.

IN THE GARDEN
We've a very good gardener here, amongst the students (Tekeu (T'kew). He worked in a nursery before he came to college and has real green fingers. He's got quite a lot of seeds coming along for us now: lettuce, cabbage, radishes, and silver beet.

ROUGH TRIP TO AITUTAKI
I want to tell you first about our recent trip to Aitutaki. The boat was awfully small, there being room for about 10 cabin passengers and 30 deck passengers. The latter were mainly Maories, who travelled all the way out on the open deck or under a tarpaulin. The ship left Rarotonga plunging at once into a very rough sea which threw the boat about from side to side and us with it. The rolling became so bad that we decided the safest place was in our bunks. I'm afraid we were all sick eventually and remained in that state for most of the journey. The journey took 26 hours instead of the normal 16 and we didn't dare look at food all the way! Disembarkation was a perilous business, as at all the outer islands, we had to climb over the fairly high side of the ship and, at a convenient moment, drop into a whale boat. This was complicated because the two boats seemed to roll in opposite directions. However, we all dropped safely. Marcus being handed from one sailor to another like a parcel.

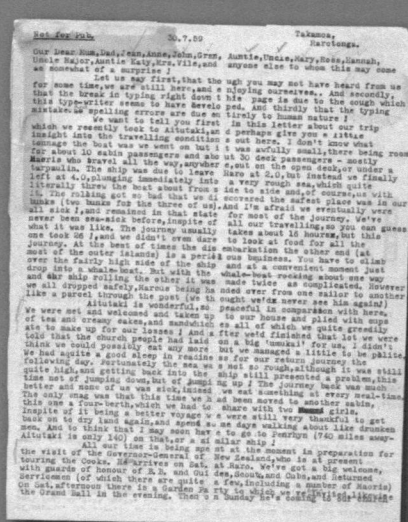

MORE ABOUT AITUTAKI

Aitutaki is wonderful. We were met and welcomed, taken up to our house, and plied with cups of tea and creamy cakes and sandwiches, all which we ate greedily, to make up for our losses! After we'd finished that lot we were told that the church people had laid on a big "umukai" for us. I didn't think we could possibly eat any more but we managed a little.

Fortunately the sea on our return was not so rough and none of us was sick; indeed we ate something at every meal time. Though it was a better voyage, we were glad to get back to dry land, where we spent some days walking about like drunken men. And to think that soon I may have to go to Penrhyn, 740 miles away compared with 140 for Aitutaki, and in the same or a similar ship!

PREPARING FOR THE GOVERNOR-GENERAL

At the moment all our time is being spent in preparing for the visit of the Governor-General of New Zealand, who is touring the Cooks. There will be a big welcome, with guards of honour of Boys' Brigade, Girl Guides, Scouts, Cubs and Returned Servicemen. On Saturday there will be a Garden Party, to which we have been invited. Likewise the Grand Ball in the evening. On Sunday he is coming to our church at Avarua. The service will be conducted by the Maori Pastor and myself, part being in English and part in Maori. We shall be lunching with the Governor at one of the Ariki's homes.

On Monday there will be cricket and rugger matches for him and the ship's crew and a big feast at Ngatangiia, laid on by all the Arikis, Mataiapos and Rangitiras of the Island. So there are dresses to be made, curtsies to be practised, bows to be performed, and the hundred-and-one other details that have to be arranged.

By the way, it seems that this is the first time that Girl Guides have attended a church service in Rarotonga, so all the church folk are pleased. He's also going to their "Uapou" (their special worship meeting) in the evening and no doubt there will be much singing, dancing and answering of questions. The poor man will probably be thoroughly worn out before he gets here; goodness knows what he'll be like when he leaves on Monday night.

LETTER FROM AUGUST 1959 – PREPARATION FOR THE NORTHERN TRIP

NORTHERN TRIP IN PROSPECT

Early next week I'm off on my Northern trip. You may remember that some time ago I mentioned that I would probably have to travel North soon to sort out a little church trouble there. Well, this is it. Unfortunately Rita cannot come as well, because we think that the journey would probably upset Marcus too much at present. I'm not going on the Dobiri, on which we went to Aitutaki, but on the Tiare which is about the same size as the Dobiri but much lower in the water. She doesn't roll, so I've been told, but when she sails into a headwind the water pours over the sides to such an extent that everything gets soaked! So I'm hoping for no headwinds. However, she is faster than the Dobiri, which is a good thing. I go first to Manihiki, 640 miles away; then to Rakahanga, 24 miles from Manihiki, and back again; then off to Penrhyn, 196 miles from Manihiki, then we return to Rarotonga via Manihiki and shall have travelled about 1720 miles. I shall probably be away for about three weeks. Three weeks with no communication with Rita except by telegram! I am not going alone. The Rev. Tua Pittman, my right-hand man here, is coming also, to translate. And Ta Upu is also hoping to go to Manihiki with us.

Tiare
Maori word meaning "flower"

INTO THE MOUNTAINS

We have been amazed to remember that we have been out of England for nearly a year. It just doesn't seem possible that time can have flown past so quickly. There is so much to do here and so many new things to see that we never seem to catch up with time. The other day, for instance, we drove up a rough beaten track into the mountains. It was beautifully peaceful. We took the car as far as we dared without letting the road ruts break the axles, and then walked. There are many lovely walks around here, if only one had the time and energy to explore them. But there is rarely time, and our energy is expended in other ways. Still we thrive on hard work and can enjoy the delights of the mountains from the back of our house, or the back of a car!

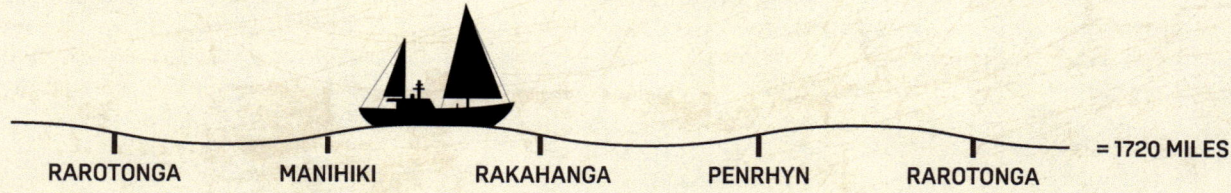

LETTERS FROM SEPTEMBER 1959 – MAORI CAROLS

PRE-TRAVEL THOUGHTS

Goodness knows what the trip will be like with this strong wind. I suppose we'll be flooded out all the way! That seems to be the usual complaint of this particular ship: in rough seas she just wallows around shipping as much water as she can hold.

PREPARING A CHRISTMAS SERVICE

I've worked out a service of nine Lessons and Carols for English Christmas service this year, giving the choir a lot more work with such things as Ding, Dong, Merrily on High, The Holly and the Ivy, The Seven Joys of Mary and Away in a Manger, all of which are quite new to them, so we're going to have a lot of fun learning them.

MARCUS

Marcus is learning all sorts of new things, all at once. His latest craze is hiding. If he's upstairs and hears one of us going up, he whispers "high, high, high" and dodges behind the curtain or under a table. Of course we have to search, though not for too long. The other day, when I went up, he desperately wanted to hide but had no time to get anywhere; so he just put his hands over his eyes! He's getting to the stage of copying everything he hears, even the language. He seems to be doing very well with his Maori; we are hoping that he will learn to speak it as quickly as English.

In an effort to keep Marcus from straying we have fixed gates everywhere; they are quite useless, though, for we've found him climbing over the 3-ft. garden wall. Also, he has discovered the fish pond, so that has had to be netted in.

He's very fond of drawing and it's agony trying to write when he is around, because he prefers my pen to a pencil. Books have always interested him, but mainly to be read upside down. Recently though, he has become interested in the pictures and can recognise many of the animals.

LETTERS FROM OCTOBER 1959 – THE NORTHERN TRIP

THE OUTWARD VOYAGE
The sea wasn't too rough but after a few hours we were all lying in our bunks. We roused ourselves for meals though these were far from appetising and most of the time I just pecked. In the cabin which also served as the saloon, library and dining room, were Tua (my right-hand man), Ta Upu Pere, a Roman Catholic Father, an old man trading salt, and myself. We looked like a motley crowd all lying around, desperately in need of a shave, reading the most appalling literature that was ever printed, sloping up odd meals and drinking thick coffee with no milk. It took us about four days to reach Penrhyn, where we arrived late on Thursday night and disembarked the next morning.

WELCOME AT PENRHYN
The local Pastor, Ben, came on board to welcome us as well as several members of the church. Not all, of course, because some belonged to the party which had broken away. On the wharf we had the usual short service – hymn, address, and prayer – and were then led away to the mission house. I was given a small room all to myself, with two single beds pushed together. It was about the most open room in the house and I felt like a naked goldfish in a bowl when I woke up in the mornings. From the front street you could see me through the French windows; from the side windows you could see me; and from the back French windows all those getting breakfast – and there were always hundreds doing just that you could see me! You either had to brazen it out and get dressed quickly or you snuggled under the bed clothes and did the best you could. I tried both methods but neither was easy.

TE TAUTUA VILLAGE

The mission house is situated right on the edge of the sea in which sharks are supposed to abound. People told me that often they can be easily caught from the back wall. One day we went eight miles across the lagoon in a sailing boat with an outboard motor to visit the other village of Te Tautua (T'towootooar) and there received a wonderful welcome. After a run of an hour and a half we arrived in the boiling hot sun. Tua and I were then led to a wooden sofa decorated with frangipani and other flower garlands. We were made to sit down on this and then the whole thing was hoisted aloft by ten strong men. It seemed as though all the strong men were my end, for I went up in the air while Tua seemed to be dragged along the ground. It may have had something to do with the difference in our weights – Tua's is about double mine!

A LOVELY CHURCH

After a couple of hundred yards we were set down at the Mission House and there welcomed by the church members who gazed at me with something like awe. We had a wonderful time there and saw the most delightful church in the whole group. It is rather dark, with lovely stained-glass windows and most beautiful wood carvings.

CATCHING A SHARK

Back in Omoka we had an Uapou (meeting with hymn-singing) on each of the three nights we were there. On Sunday I had to preach at the morning service. Ta preached at the afternoon service and Tua conducted the Uapou. After the latter we went off to see a fishing boat that had just come in with about 200 flying fish. Some of these we cut up and threw over the mission wall to attract the sharks and soon they came, though only small ones, about two feet long. One of these we hooked and I helped to pull the line in, so they all said I had caught my first shark!

NO CALENDARS ON PENRHYN

After many meetings we healed the split and left everyone in a happy and friendly mood of Christian fellowship. On Monday morning we sailed for Manihiki, absolutely loaded with gifts from individuals and the churches, including some real pearls. I was sorry to leave Penrhyn; it is such a lovely island, and I don't mind having to live there for six months or so, any time. I would be sorry for Rita though, for there is really nothing to do all day long. The people seem to recognise no calendars, clocks or watches and it can be rather delightful if you have plenty to keep you busy.

INCIDENTS ON THE TRIP TO MANIHIKI

Our trip from Penrhyn to Manihiki was great fun. It is normally an overnight trip but it took us two full days. First of all a bearing went in the engine and we had to use a sail for about four or five hours. Then a privately owned whaleboat which we were towing went adrift. Enquiries made as soon as it was missed showed that it was last seen about an hour before so we had to turn round and go back to look for it. By this time the seas were quite high and I doubted whether it would still be afloat but after about ten minutes it turned up, apparently none the worse. Some hours after this the cook fell overboard! He had been peeling potatoes over the side and as the ship gave an extra lurch a rather large wave which broke over us took him off as well. Fortunately someone had been watching him and we soon had him back on board, still clutching his peeling knife! He didn't seem to mind his soaking; I should have been scared stiff, what with the high seas and the probability of sharks.

AT MANIHIKI

At last we got to Manihiki. We had to go ashore in canoes as the passage is not deep enough for anything larger. It was great fun to be riding through the surf and narrowly missing the sharp-pointed coral rocks only a few inches below the surface.

We were welcomed by a small guard of honour of the Boys' Brigade and Girl Guides and passed through them to the mission house which, with the church, is right on the sea shore. After a short service, a cup of tea, and a rest, I was taken off by the Pastor to inspect the school, walking through each classroom, meeting the teachers, and seeing the children all busy at their lessons. In the evening there was an Uapou. The singing in the northern islands is quite different from that in the southern group. It's still somewhat like a chant but the expression marks in the music are made by dropping or raising the singing half a semitone or so.

A STONE MONUMENT

The next morning, after sleeping in a large double bed, Tua and I went off with a few others to a village, two miles distant, on the other side of the lagoon. We went in a sailing boat – but this one had no motor. With a good wind we got there in three quarters of an hour and made the return journey in half an hour. I inspected the church and a rather special stone monument where the Gospel is supposed to have first been preached on that island. It is quite an impressive stone rather like one would imagine the altar that Elijah set up when challenging the prophets of Baal. Indeed I believe that that was the first text preached here. After a good lunch we went back across the lagoon and then tried to settle the trouble in the main village of Tauhunu ("Towhoonoo"). We were not so successful there. The party that has walked out of the church still refuses to return until they have a new Pastor.

ADRIFT OFF AITUTAKI
We left Manihiki in the evening, again laden with gifts from the two churches. With quite rough seas we had a long slow journey to Aitutaki where we had to stop to take on the mail and a passenger. We arrived about 8pm, after dark, and after waiting in vain for the launch to come out to the ship we put out to sea a little way and anchored for the night. When morning came we found we had drifted miles and it took two hours of hard going to get back to the island. No one had kept watch during the night or they would have noticed our drift. When the launch eventually came out we discovered that they had seen us the night before and had come out, but as we kept drifting away they returned to land.

THE SEA'S FINAL FLING
It was very rough between Aitutaki and Rarotonga, with great waves breaking right over our saloon. We had a crowded saloon too, with twice the proper number of passengers – all Maoris except me. My bunk was lying crosswise to the direction of the ship and as it rolled about I kept drifting from one end to the other, several times only just saving myself from sliding right out. There were no sides to any of the bunks and throughout the night I had to sleep while hanging on with one arm over my head, grabbing the top of the bunk. It is not surprising that I woke up as early as 5am. I didn't mind, though, because by then Rarotonga was in view. It was wonderful to see it again.

RAROTONGA WELCOME
We eventually landed and Rita and Marcus were both waiting on the quay. I wondered whether he would remember me, or suddenly go all shy. However he put his little face up for a kiss at once and all was well. I rolled about for most of that day, still imagining that I was on the ship, and Marcus rolled everywhere with me, he just wouldn't let me out of his sight. It was good to get home; it felt as if I had been away for two and a half months, instead of weeks.

MIDWIFERY UNDER DIFFICULTIES

I thought you would be amused at one of the odd happenings to me while John was away. I was awakened just after midnight one night by violent banging on the bedroom door and the senior student and his wife shouting, "Come quickly, Mama; Mareta is having her baby outside." I rushed like a streak of sleepy lightning to Mareta's house but was a couple of minutes too late to be of any real help; the baby had just arrived on the path outside the house. The poor thing was lying on the gravel and no-one had thought to wrap her up; they were all concerned with the mother. This mother has had a bit of trouble during her pregnancy and I thought it rather important for her to get to hospital in case there were any complications. Also, I thought the baby might need extra care after her exposure to the night air and cold ground. So I grabbed a blanket and wrapped the child up and fled back here to the phone. I couldn't even get the exchange – I think the man must have been asleep – so I sent Tei (Tay) to the hospital in the car while I went back to Mareta who by this time had taken herself and the babe into the house. I found the baby was still all muddled up with her cord and after-birth. I straightened her out and put some of Marcus's cot sheets on and around her, still thinking of treatment for shock. The nurse eventually came back with Tei, cut the cord, left Mum to look after herself, and that was that. As this was Mareta's ninth child I suppose the nurse thought she was quite able to look after herself. Two days later they were home again!!

The doctors were amused at the story and when they found that Mareta hadn't a name for her baby. Mareta asked me to suggest a name and I wrote down several I liked leaving the final choice to them. They chose "Teremoana" for two reasons – first because it was on my list, and second because the name means "to travel by sea" – which John was doing at that time. Maoris like to give names associated with special events. Teremoana, by the way, is a very common Island name.

God bless you both. Love Rita xx

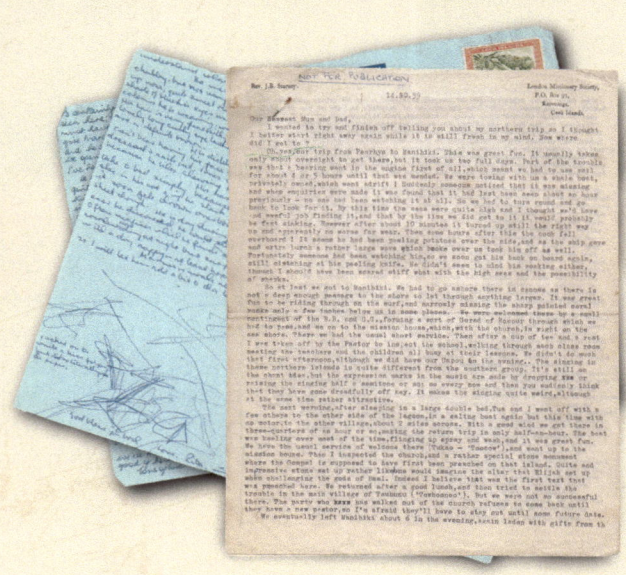

DUST

Really you'd hardly believe the amount of dust that can collect on a car out here, mind you, we've not had any real rain for over a fortnight so driving on the roads behind any vehicle is like going through a London fog! The handbrake hasn't worked recently and I discovered, the other day, that this was because the mechanism under the car was absolutely covered with dried mud! Not much chance of a car in Aitutaki, I'm afraid, though we might try persuading the L.M.S. to splash out on a Vespa.

MARCUS

Marcus plays quite happily by himself with his bricks for quite a long time. He looked so funny after lunch today wandering in and out of the verandah carrying bricks, with his own B.B. hat jammed down on his head at a crazy angle. He still loves the car of course and always has to come out whenever we go anywhere. He also likes helping. This afternoon I was giving the car a dust over and he had to get the brace for the wheel nuts and go round trying to tighten them all up.

LETTER FROM NOVEMBER 1959 – HAPPY BIRTHDAY MARCUS

Your grandson is now well and truly two years old. He had a wonderful birthday. The first present he opened was a matchbox car and his eyes nearly fell out of his head. He got crafty from then with his gifts, anything feeling a bit soft and most unlike a car he let well alone; but if it rattled or seemed to have wheels it had to be opened straight away without any nonsense. In the afternoon he had a birthday party. Rita made a lovely birthday tea, with jellies, blancmanges, fruit salad, egg sandwiches, fancy iced cakes, and iced biscuits, and the piece-de-resistance his birthday cake in the shape of a ship with two funnels, masts, and sea.

Happy 2nd Birthday Marcus!

LETTER FROM DECEMBER 1959 – FESTIVITIES

CHOIR CHRISTMAS EVE PARTY
We've got loads of plans under way already for what we're hoping to do, not only with ourselves but also with the students. There will be a Christmas Eve party for the choir and the students. I ought to explain this mysterious "Choir". This is the Maori choir which makes the music for the English Service on Sunday evenings. There are 60 people, but only about 40 are usually present. They are a great asset to our service. Our party is an altervative to all manner of cocktail parties on Christmas Eve. It keeps them off the bottle and gives them a good time.

CHRISTMAS PRESENT-GIVING
We're planning to have chicken for our Christmas dinner. Chicken is the most common meat meal here, had at every umukai and special feast, but we don't feel we can go without it on Christmas Day. Rita has also made the Christmas puddings and cake, and they've turned out a real treat, so much so that just to smell them makes my mouth water already. We've invited all the students, wives and children up to the house after dinner for their presents. We've wrapped them all in separate little parcels and shall hang them on the tree. After a carol, we'll get some of the smaller children to hand them round.

SWIMMING POOL
Today we had an airmail post from Aitutaki and received some lovely letters. Thank you for Marcus's birthday present, a paddling pool. He was thrilled, and so were we! You would have laughed to see Rita and me on Sunday morning, decked out in our costumes and sitting in Marcus's pool, and with Marcus running round and squirting the hose on us! You could not have bought him anything nicer; we had been saying that we wished we could have got him his own swimming pool – and then it turned up – so unexpectedly that we almost believe in miracles.

LETTERS FROM JANUARY 1960 – NEW YEAR THOUGHTS

A STRANGE NEW YEAR SERVICE
What a wonderful Christmas we've had, although, of course, very rushed. New Year was also a very busy time. On New Year's Eve we went round the villages here, giving a little greeting to everyone – and all in Maori, Rita included. I had to leave Rita at 11.45pm and go and meet the local pastor of Avarua. With him and quite a good number of young people, I went to the local dance hall, where there was a giddy dance in progress, made more giddy by a number of drunks. There we had arranged to take a service. You would have been amazed if you had been there. As soon as the pastor called for silence and announced a hymn, there was complete quiet; people just stood where they were and sang. Then he gave a very short reading and I followed with a prayer again in Maori, and then we left. It really was a most strange experience to go into a public dance, stop the dancing, hold a short service in which you could hear a pin drop, and leave them to carry on with their festivities. I don't think it would be possible for that to happen in many other places in the world.

SHACK BREAK
We went on a little break to the shack again and had a wonderful time. When we go now we certainly do it in style. We take the primus stove and make fresh tea and fill the car up with every possible want for at least a week! We get Marcus to sleep sometime during the day and then we go in for a swim. Yesterday we had two, one on our own and one with him. He certainly does love the water. He likes floating on his front now, being held up of course, but he really thinks he's swimming.

WEEK OF PRAYER
A new student and his wife arrived last Sunday and we've had a busy time preparing for them. Also this week is our Week of Prayer which means that I have to be up at 5am each morning for the service at 5.30am! This year the week is based on the Lord's Prayer, thinking about one or two different phrases each day.

HOT AND HUMID
We're in the hot, humid, hurricane season now. The temperature often isn't very high, not much over 78°C, but it feels as if it ought to be registering 88°C. It makes one very hot and sticky and it's tempting to throw off all the bedclothes at night – only to wake up later and find it's really cold. Perhaps that's how Rita got her cold – a real snorter, but she's still up and about, can't keep her down!

YOUR TIME, AND OURS
A few Sundays ago we said how strange it was to think of you – at home getting ready for church, wrapping up in furs and gloves, and so on, while we were in whites and cotton dresses. Sometimes that other part of the world, where you are living, seems quite unreal, as if everything there has stopped, and won't start up again until we're home. When you're coming out of evening service at home we're just putting the finishing touches to our getting ready for the first service of the day.

"The voice of prayer is never silent."

MARCUS
Marcus often comes up with me to feed them, shouting out something about the fissssshhhhssssshhyyyy, except when he's feeling specially obstreperous; then he calls them "ships". He's using a terrific lot of Maori now and I feel sometimes that he's having a jolly good laugh when we can't understand. Of course at other times it must be frustrating to have two dim-witted parents who can't even understand a simple language like Maori.

FISH POND
At the moment of typing there's a dragonfly floating laboriously round the lamp and I'm expecting any moment to get dive bombed by it. Things that in England we thought were only for the garden and lily pond come right into the house here and become perfect nuisances. Did we ever tell you, by the way, that we've a fish pond here? I've no idea what kind of fish they are, but they're supposed to be fed on the left-over toast after breakfast. It's an awful job trying to remember. Sometimes I suddenly realise that they've not been fed for four or five days, and they then get a huge meal. They don't seem to grow very big which I suppose, with their erratic meals, isn't surprising. They're here to supplement the ration when fishing isn't particularly good in the lagoons, but at the moment they'd be better popped into a sardine tin.

ANNUAL CAMPS
Tomorrow is the beginning of the Boys' Brigade, Guide Guide, and Life Boy camps, all in different villages so for the rest of this week I'll be busy flying from one camp to the next and appearing at this, that, and the other - anything from flag-hoisting to camp-firing. It won't be much fun this year because the car is not in good order. The front wheels need greasing, and the steering wheel feels like a ton of bricks when we turn a corner. Fortunately there aren't many corners to turn on Rarotonga.

ONE LAW FOR ONE AND ONE LAW FOR ANOTHER
Some time ago they wanted to put up a proper licensed hotel here, to attract tourists. We get far too many as it is for they're not helping the people here to understand the meaning of the western way of life. So often it seems to them that there's one law for the white people and a different, more rigid, one for the Maoris. For example the Press very often reports Maoris who are fined for brewing or consuming drink, but there is never a similar reference to a European, though he does just the same thing. Of course the latter is more cunning. A European will never be allowed by his friends to walk out along the public roads if he's drunk, so he's never seen. But there are many Europeans here who quite blatantly walk into one of the stores here and, in front of everyone, order all the ingredients for making home-brewed beer.

THE SOCIAL ROUND
Not all are like this, of course. One New Zealander, who just arrived, is a strong Boys' Brigade officer from Nelson, captain of the company. We're hoping we can give him some sort of work in the companies here. I fear, though, that he may not stay more than his contract term of three years, because any New Zealander who doesn't drink or join in with the social round of the Administration people is not well liked, gets very lonely and despondent, and usually gives up. This sounds morbid, but it's not really as bad as it sounds. Of course the fact that the missionary doesn't drink or join quite so much in the social round doesn't ostracise him. He is made a friend of by most of the Administrative hierarchy because he can do more than they can with the Maoris.

MORE ABOUT THE CAMPS
The interval in this letter is due to last-minute preparations for the Camps. The Life Boys are camping in Avarua school, next door to Takamoa, so they're easy to visit. They have 17 boys and seven officers in camp including our one-and-only lady Life Boys leader. They have planned a lot of games and sports as well as a visit to the Freezer and the Printing Works. They are also to have some swimming, a Parents' Day, and a Film Show.

The Boys' Brigade are camping in the school at Arorangi. They've got about 80 boys in camp – a small number when you realise that one company alone, that at Avarua, has 80 boys alone and that there are 5 other companies in Rarotonga. It looks as though they'll enjoy themselves.

The Guides are out at Titikaveka. It's usual for them to camp in the same village as the Boys' Brigade camp and we thought that a little too near, so they took themselves off to the next village. They have about 60 girls in camp.

NOTHING ON AITUTAKI
I think we're in for a bit of a shock when we get to Aitutaki, after having started life out here on Rarotonga. We shall have no running water, no electricity, no proper roads, only a handful of Europeans, no European doctor, no school for English speaking children, no shack, no sailing club, no bowling green, no cinemas for Europeans, very little English food, no fresh meat except chicken, no freezer, no car, no hotel, and so on.

ANOTHER HURRICANE IN NIUE
Yesterday we had news of a second hurricane in Niue. It seems that both the church and the mission house have been destroyed and all the plants which were just recovering from the one they had this time last year.

Fortunately the hurricane has moved south so will miss us. However we're prepared if one comes here, with great thick ropes strung right over the roof of this house. This is supposed to be one of the safety zones.

LETTERS FROM FEBRUARY 1960 – QUICK UPDATE

BERNARD'S RETURN DELAYED
We've heard that Bernard is not going to be back as soon as we thought. We had a telegram the other day saying that he won't be here as soon as expected as he's going to Niue for one month; I presume to give a bit of moral support after this second hurricane. We've been keyed up for going to our real permanent home on Aitutaki, and knowing we may well have to wait until perhaps June is a bit trying.

YOUTH FELLOWSHIP'S PRESENT
Kingston Youth Fellowship sent us a lovely present the other day – a 3D Viewmaster with slides of England, Austria, Snow White and the Nativity. It was so unexpected, and no fuss, either; just a little card saying "with best wishes from the Y.F." We were tremendously thrilled and that evening I had to take it to the students and show the slides of London.

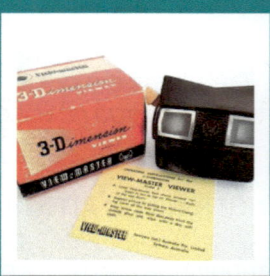

EYES ON A PIANO
We've at last got our eyes on a piano! A couple who have been here two years are having to leave soon because of the wife's health. They've only just bought this piano from a returned-home resident and when we heard they were leaving we asked them to give us the first option to buy it, to which they agreed. It's not yet "in the bag" though, as they have just discovered that they may have to pay their own fare back to England, in which case the price of the piano will rocket considerably.

MARCH 1960 – PREPARING TO LEAVE RAROTONGA

AT THE SHACK AGAIN
We have come out to the shack again. We have decided that the break will do us good and as we have the car we can pop back to Avarua whenever we want to. We've been here a week and have benefited enormously. There has been plenty of rain, though, and strong winds. The second night we were woken by a pitiful cry from Marcus and on investigating discovered that the rain was leaking through the roof and down onto his head! So he spent the rest of the night in our bed, much to his delight. However yesterday and today we've seen the sun at last.

UNINTENTIONAL SWIM
We went swimming yesterday, not on purpose. We had borrowed an outrigger canoe and were going to try to get across the lagoon to the reef. Half way there the wretched thing began to fill with water rapidly and we scrambled out just as it went under water. Fortunately it didn't actually sink and as we were in swimming clothes it didn't matter a lot. We had to swim pushing this great boat-load of water back until we found a convenient head of coral on which we could stand and try to empty it out.

THE PRIEST AND THE RAT
We've had fun in the evenings here. We've discovered there must be a nest of rats somewhere in the roof and all of them, mother, father and about four babies, come down and visit us each night. They're jolly daring, too. They run right along behind your chair where you're sitting or sit out in the middle of the floor staring balefully at you, almost daring you to throw a shoe. Last night we had even greater excitement. The Roman Catholic Father across the way from us came in for a cup of tea. And suddenly one of the baby rats ran up under his cassock! Poor man, I'm not sure who was the more scared, for he danced up and down trying to shake it out and when it fell it went off like a shot. However the Father stayed on for another hour so he couldn't have minded too much.

LONGING FOR AITUTAKI
We have heard that the Thorogoods hope to get back here in late April or early May. We're hoping it will be as soon as possible as we're longing to get to Aitutaki and be settled in our own home. It will be the very first one of our own since we were married, so you can imagine our excitment.

BEGINNING TO PACK UP
The pace is really steaming up a bit now as we've only got about another month here before we go over to Aitutaki. So again we are in the throes of packing up, though this time it doesn't have to be done quite so seriously. We've still got all our packing cases intact except one which I made into very necessary food safes. Most of the heavy furniture will probably go over unpacked – simply wrapped in mats. Added to the steaming pace is also the steaming weather, with temperatures well up in the 80s most of the while.

THE PIANO ARRIVES
Yesterday, not only did we have the post, bringing your letters, but we also received our piano. I had great fun, in the few odd spare minutes, playing it. Unfortunately a meeting in the afternoon prevented me from getting to it, and in the evening we had a tea put on by the choir for our organist who is leaving this week, so there wasn't much time for piano-playing.

WE ORGANISE A DANCE
There were so many people who we wanted to invite up for dinner here before we left, and suddenly Rita had the idea of an informal dance. We had terrific fun preparing for it, though the food preparation wasn't exactly "fun" for Rita. Everything went off almost better than we could have hoped. We had about 36 people in our Lecture Room which had been decorated with bamboo, frangipani, and coconuts ready to drink, and the way to the Hall was lit by blazing bamboo torches. The students put on a little cabaret for us and everybody went away absolutely thrilled. Particularly so, I think, because we had proved that this sort of thing could be done without beer or spirits.

EASTER CONFERENCE PLANNED

We have in preparation at the moment an Easter Conference for the young people and are trying to run it on much the same lines as the old Easter Schools. About 70 young people, aged between 15 and 25, want to come although at first we thought there would be only a dozen or so. The problem, for Rita, will be eating and sleeping. We can probably put all the girls in the Lecture Hall, while the boys go down to the Sunday School Hall. The conference will run from Thursday to Easter Sunday evening so that we can have a break ourselves on Easter Monday.

PROGRAMME OF COLLEGE LECTURES

Lecture work still goes on at much the same pace as ever. This year I'm lecturing on the New Testament, Book of Revelation; Old Testament, the History of the Jews up to the Exile. Systematic Theology will deal with Our Belief in God, and Church History on the Different Forms of Church Government. In addition there are the usual English lessons – pronunciation and grammar, and tutorials morning and afternoons. A little easier this term, of course, as I shall only be doing it for about ten weeks.

I've just set the students their afternoon work – clearing out and packing up cases for our move, cutting firewood for the kitchen and tidying the garden. They work at this from 1 till 3 and then have an hour's study period. Then I have someone coming to talk to me about the Boys' Brigade and their bands, and after that we're off to our afternoon tea.

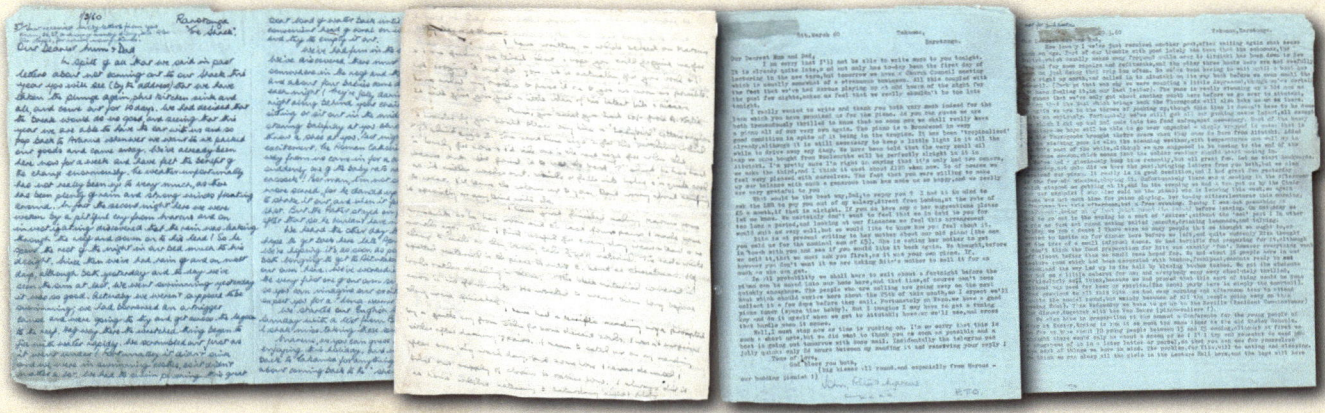

April 1960 – The Ever Growing Easter Conference

CRAWLING INSECT EATS WOOLIES

Wooly things would be most acceptable for birthday or Christmas presents. We are particularly short at the moment, mainly due to ignorance on my part. I now know to my cost that we have a nasty little crawling insect which creeps into everything and makes hundreds of little holes. I was nearly heartbroken a little while ago when I got out the trunk for our warmer things. I've certainly learnt a lesson, and everything not in actual use is smothered in moth crystals.

EASTER CONFERENCE PREPARATIONS

We are now up to our eyes in Easter Conference arrangements. Originally we expected no more than 50 and nearly had a fit when over 120 returns poured in. Feeding them is the biggest headache, finding big enough saucepans, but we're hoping Avarua members will help out.

Here is a list of what the youngsters must bring:- 1 plate and 1 cup, tin of taro, tin of meat, and mattress. The last item sounds a bit odd, but the Maoris are used to taking them to camp, or when holidaying with friends. 38 children are taking special parts in the Conference - 10 Group Leaders, 10 Reports, 6 for Morning and Evening Prayers, and 12 to serve Communion. As far as we know, this is the first conference of this particular kind and it is causing great excitement. We would like to see it become an annual event, of course. That will be our aim for Aitutaki at least.

EASTER CONFERENCE PLANS

The other day we had a meeting of what I call the Junior Conference Staff for this Easter. Of the 38 due, 35 actually came, very encouraging. If the weather is fine at Easter we're going to try a big open-air Communion Service on Good Friday afternoon. Morning Prayers, taken by the young people themselves, will also be out in the open if the weather is good, but the lectures will have to be inside, in the Lecture Room. I would like them to be in the open air but we have decided that if the weather is good, it will probably be so good that all the young people will go to sleep in the sun! I've not discovered how we are going to crowd 120 into the Lecture Room but no doubt we'll manage somehow. I've got Ta and another pastor here, Tua, to help me with the lectures, so we'll have a proper Conference Staff.

HELP FROM THE ISLANDERS
I shall never cease to be thankful to the old Easter Schools for all that they taught me; but we didn't realise before what a lot of hard work was involved in them. Many people, in different ways, have been very good about the conference. One man has promised firewood and a sack of flour; another gave us £1 to be used in any way that was needed, and so we've gone on. I feel sorry for Rita, of course, with all the headache of food and sleeping and washing and toilets and so on. But she is doing it extremely well and in a very businesslike way, so the team work of planning is going forward well.

OFF TO AITUTAKI SOON
New pen, new writing, new person! Today we have had a telegram from the Thorogoods to say that they will be on the next Maui, due here at the end of this month. We're thrilled that we know something definite at last. The only disappointment is that the Maui is not going on to Aitutaki so that we shall have to trust ourselves to a rolling journey over in a local schooner as soon after they arrive as we can. We've already shipped five packing cases of odds and ends, papers, ornaments and small furniture. Most of the actual packing we've left to students who have made a first-rate job of it. Much of the bigger furniture will have to be done up in sacks and mats.

THE THOROGOODS RETURN
This must now be the last letter from Rarotonga, as on Monday we leave on our dear friend the Dobiri for our new home. On Wednesday the Thorogoods returned and we were happy to see them once again. We had been told that the Maui was due to come in at 4.30pm so we dutifully went down to the wharf, only to find that the ship was nowhere in sight. We waited for a bit but then decided to leave a student down at the wharf to let us know as soon as the ship was in sight. At about 5.30pm he came puffing up to the house to tell us that the Maui was already tied up, so we rushed down again. This time we were greeted by a sign on the shipping company offices to say that the passengers would not be coming off until 7pm! And all this time we had a large reception ready and waiting to greet the Thorogoods up at Takamoa. We had lined the walk right up to the house with boys and girls from the Boys' Brigade and Girl Guides, with the students standing right by the house steps.

The Thorogoods

Well, at last 7pm came and the first boat-load of goods started to come off, but not the passengers. We had to wait till nearly 8pm for them. Rita and I and Glassie, the Church Secretary were especially privileged, and allowed to wait down at the end of the wharf to greet the Thorogoods as they arrived. The rest of the people, even those waiting for husbands or wives had to wait behind the barrier at the other end, so we felt very honoured. But this is just an example of the high regard in which the L.M.S. is held here.

Of course they were very tired, so after greeting hundreds of people down at the wharf we managed to drive them home. They had to walk down the rows of patiently waiting boys and girls, who by this time had lit bamboo torches to light the way, and as the Thorogoods walked up they sang them a greeting song which they had made up specially for the occasion. They were both piled up high with "eis", reaching pretty well up to the tops of their heads, and how they could still see, I just don't know.

We came indoors and had a short rest while Rita settled Marcus, who had been down on the wharf with us all that while. We had to keep him there as we had promised him all day long that we would show him the big boat, and I think he was duly sobered and impressed. When all was quiet we went in for prayers to the Chapel and almost immediately afterwards we went over to the Lecture Room for a feast which the students had prepared. A bit late in the day for eating, but it was all good, and great fun.

EASTER CONFERENCE A SUCCESS

The Conference was a great success, I think, and everything went off very smoothly. We've a long way to go before the tradition of our Easter School is built but this has made a very good start. Now we'll have to start all over again in Aitutaki with our next Easter.

FAREWELL FEASTS

We have already begun our round of farewells. On Monday the students, quite out of the blue, laid on a farewell feast for us, and gave us presents! This was almost unexpected and we were thrilled. We received a pair of rope sandals for reef fishing, several cushion covers, a pillow-case beautifully hand-embroidered by one of the students' wives, some shells, and a single bed "tivaivai". Marcus had a little basket specially made for his size. It really was lovely of them to do all this. In the evening we went to dinner with the Treasurer and spent a pleasant evening there.

On Tuesday at 4pm we had a proper English dinner prepared by the Pastor at Nikau. Do you recall that when we arrived he had prepared the church there to give us a feast on English lines, even including waiters with serviettes over their arms? This was that same place and it certainly was a lovely meal. We had to rush away to get back to a young European couple recently married here, for another evening meal! You can imagine how full we were after the first; however, we managed to be very polite and eat this other food also! The evening there was made for us by the showing of some coloured slides of their visit to London. They were both in the London Police Force and the wife had been stationed at the police houses in Roehampton! It was lovely to see the slides of Regent Street all lit up at night at Christmas time, and the tree in Trafalgar Square, and so on. It really made us feel that we still belonged to London.

PACKING

All of last week and a good deal of this have been spent in packing. We discover that for this move over to Aitutaki we have at least 36 packets and boxes and parcels and goodness-knows-what! You can see that in this short while we have been doing a lot of collecting. We were very thankful on Wednesday morning to see it all loaded onto the Dobiri, ready for sailing on Monday. The students have worked like Trojans throughout this time, not only carting cases and boxes everywhere, but also doing a good share of the actual packing.

We are terribly thrilled at the moment at the thought of being in our own home, with our own furniture and so on. We've got a new water tank going over. This will be set up high and the water pumped into it from the lower tank so that we have some pressure for the lavatory cistern and the shower. Meanwhile, of course, we have to help the Thorogoods unpack and talk over a whole year's work together.

LETTERS FROM MAY 1960 – WE HAVE ARRIVED

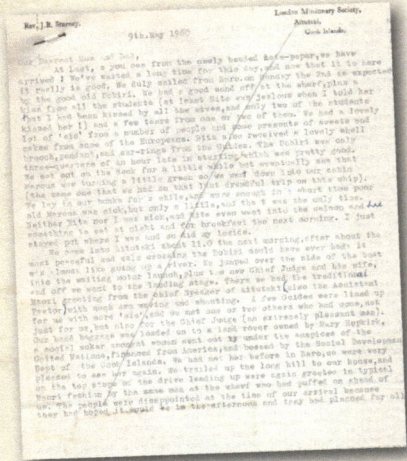

OFF TO AITUTAKI
As you see from the newly headed notepaper, we have arrived! We've waited a long time for this day and now that it's here, it really is good. We sailed from Rarotonga by the good old Dobiri. Had a good send-off from the wharf, plus a kiss from all the students. Rita was jealous when I told her I had been kissed by all the wives, and only two of the students had kissed her! We had some presents of sweets and cakes from some of the Europeans. Rita also received a lovely shell brooch, pendant and ear-rings from the Guides. We sat out on deck for a while but eventually saw that Marcus was turning a little green, so we went down into our cabin – the same one that we had on that last dreadful trip on this ship.

BEGINNING AGAIN AT AITUTAKI
It is so long since many of you received any direct word from us that this letter must read as a message from beyond the grave! We are in Aitutaki and limbering up for the real work for which we were sent. Aitutaki ("Eye-two-tucky") is 140 miles north of Rarotonga, a short distance along your latest M1 roadway, but to us a vast journey when taken in a light schooner over an endless expanse of ocean. We had a calm crossing taking only 20 hours. We were greeted with garlands of flowers from the Girl Guides, a welcome call from the Assistant Pastor of the main church at Arutanga, a delightful old character called Monga, but suffering from filaria in both legs, a handshake from the Chief of Police and a handshake from the Resident Agent. The latter two were not really present for us alone, but had come to greet the new Chief Judge from Rarotonga, and his wife, who had travelled over with us. The Resident Agent on each island is permitted to try court cases for which the penalty does not exceed 12 months in prison; for anything over that the Chief Judge must be called in.

A HOME ON THE HILL

We trailed up the long hill to our house, and on the top steps of the drive we were again greeted in typical Maori fashion by the same man who was at the wharf and had puffed on ahead of us. The people were disappointed at the time of our arrival; they had hoped it would be in the afternoon and had planned for all the Guides and Boys' Brigade, together with their band, to be on parade at the wharf.

Well, we came into the house and the first thing we saw was some new lino in the sitting room. We explored further, and found lino also in our bedroom and also in my study, and all specially for us! One or two of the mission houses on Rarotonga are beginning to get lino down on the floors and Rita and Janette were only saying the other day, what a pity it was, when they could weave some beautiful mats themselves at hardly any cost. Fortunately the lino in the sitting room couldn't have been a better choice in colour. It is grey with red and yellow flowers on it and it matches up well with our grey three-piece and the yellow curtains that Rita has made for the windows. The lino in the other rooms is green with yellow and red roses on it. Rita had already planned red curtains for the bedroom so it really doesn't look bad at all.

SETTLING IN

We've not done a thing this whole week except unpack and arrange things. Towards the end of the week we were held up because we had nowhere to put any more things. So I started on the large cupboard for the kitchen in which we hope to hide a multitude of things. I've got it standing upright today, and tomorrow I hope to fix it to the wall, so that I can remove the present rather unsafe shelves in the kitchen which hold all our crockery and glassware, and use them for bookcases in my study.

We were presented with four chickens the other day. We only have three now because Pastor Sam's son, a boy of Marcus's age, un-tied one, and it was never seen again. So today we had to get a boy along to build a pen out of roofing iron, and Rita expertly cut the wings of the remaining three. I never imagined that one day I would be hanging on to a chicken while its wings were being cut! It's something they don't warn you about before you become a missionary.

WELCOME FEASTS

On the first day we had a feast prepared by the Aitutaki deacons and Church Council. We had to wait until 3pm for this but when it came, it was worth waiting for – a whole roast pig! We felt as if we had gone back to Christmas in the Middle Ages. On Wednesday, the people of Arutanga gave us another feast; on Thursday the people of Vaipai did the same, and on Friday the rest of the Tautu people brought their contributions.

For the month the churches and districts are taking it in turn to supply us with uncooked food. At pretty much every meal so far we've had to eat chicken so, as you can imagine, roast beef would be a real treat. But no fresh meat is obtainable in Aitutaki so we live on chicken, fish, and corned beef!

NEARLY WINTER BUT 78

We've found a housegirl so Rita is very busy at the moment trying to train her and trying to keep patience when things go wrong, both of which she's doing admirably. We are now in the beginning of winter. Part of the cause of this is using a kerosene lamp by which to type. These lamps throw out a powerful heat so most nights it seems just as hot as in the day. If you could see me now, you would think I must have gotten more and more untidy in my old age. I am surrounded by books, papers, souvenirs, stationery, boxes, parcels, and hundreds of odds and ends. But I'm stuck for the moment for anywhere to put all the stuff. I only hope that no-one decides to pay me an official visit!

Arutanga CICC, Aitutaki 2023

FIRST SUNDAY

I had to preach at the Arutanga church. This is the church with the pulpit in the middle against a wall and congregation to the left and right. The Boys' Brigade and Guides turned up in force – a most unheard of thing when it is not their parade day. After dinner we went up to Mary Hopkins' for a quiet afternoon, finishing up with a drive round the island in her land rover and a supper of scrambled egg.

SHORTAGE OF WATER

The piano is a great success. Yesterday I spent most of the evening thoroughly enjoying myself with it. I had it tuned before leaving Rarotonga and enquired about putting a lamp in it here, to keep out the damp. However they suggested that I would need nothing because the climate here is much dryer than in Rarotonga. We are coming into the dry season now, when we have three months without any rain. Then washing is down to the minimum, the lavatory cistern pulled only when absolutely necessary, and a shower only when all three can stand under it together. The shower water at present smells of petrol as the tank water has to be pumped up to two petrol drums - recently installed to give sufficient pressure.

MARCUS

Marcus has settled down extremely well. He plays all day long with Sam's children, of which they have four at home and another five planted out at different places. Today he went over to Sam's and came back with the tiniest kitten I've seen, tightly gripping it by the neck! He had another thrill today when he was allowed to carry the clipped chickens over to their new pen.

You should have seen him gingerly walking across the grass carrying a huge chicken and talking to the head which kept popping up to look at him. He talks nineteen to the dozen now, mostly in Maori, but with enough English for us to get the gist of what he's saying. He gets most bashful if he makes a mistake. When we were at Mary's yesterday he was asked to bring me an ashtray and instead he brought me a book. When he found his mistake, he couldn't look at anyone for a good few minutes. He has terrific energy and is continually rushing about all over the place; he has a voice like a foghorn, mainly reserved for use when we have company. When he's singing, as at prayer time at night, his voice is very light and quite good.

TALE OF AN OPENED ROAD
We've been very thrilled today. When I took over from Bernard there was an old road actually running right through the centre of Takamoa in Rarotonga, but not in use for many years.

Then the Government wanted to open it up, and there was little we could do, as it wasn't our property. Shortly after Bernard left the road was duly opened and in time came into great use by store trucks, motor bikes, private cars, and so on. Now, I understand that it was only to be used by tractors and in the event of an emergency, such as a hurricane when the sea road would be blocked. So I wrote to the Deputy Resident Commissioner when the R.C. was on furlough and received back a stinking letter saying that once a road is a public road, it could not be restricted in any way. Well the other day I mentioned all this to the Resident Commissioner and he said he saw no reason why it should not be restricted by the Island Council to tractors and any emergency. Today the Island Council met and after about half-an-hour's argument it was agreed, though by no means unanimously, to restrict the use of the road. We're thrilled at having won this battle. Of course the battle was not only for the convenience of Takamoa, but also for all the L.M.S. Islanders, who regard the whole property as being rather sacred ground. Certainly the original decision to open the road had upset many of them.

THE TIDAL WAVE
I am sorry if the newspapers made you anxious about us. In fact we knew nothing about the tidal wave at all until a couple of days later when we heard all about the Chile disaster and that the wave had been felt at Rarotonga, though doing no damage. Apparently it came on Sunday night, washed the water in and out of the harbours there and broke two visiting yachts. We pride ourselves in Aitutaki on our safety here. The house is set way up on a hill overlooking the harbour so that no tidal wave could reach us. But we could have a wonderful view of one, if it ever came.

AT THE MOVIES
A fortnight ago we went to the pictures! The people at the airport have them once a fortnight when the TEAL plane brings them. Mary collected us and several others and we thoroughly enjoyed ourselves.

CARPENTRY

I've been making things for the home out of packing cases! Sounds awful, but if you have a plane the wood comes out quite well. I've finished a kitchen cabinet except for painting and fixing the doors. We received our new stainless steel sink unit top so I spent most of the afternoon making legs for that and tomorrow I shall start on the underneath cupboards. I've also got some plans for some bedroom furniture consisting of a corner wardrobe flanked on either side by small cupboards. I've just finished making a swing and a slide for Marcus so that there is something in the garden to keep him at home – he's taken to wandering off with the pastor's children. I've also made some shelves for my study.

OUR NEW HOME

We arrived at our house, a distance of only a quarter of a mile from the wharf, but uphill all the way. This does mean that we have a most glorious view from our front verandah overlooking the wharf and anchorage, but it also means a climb of 60 steep steps before our verandah is reached. The house was in beautiful condition, for the three churches on Aitutaki had put in a lot of time and energy and money to make it just right for us. Three rooms have been covered in lino – a very new craze amongst the Maori people and the house repainted; walls whitewashed and wood-work a dark green. The house has been furnished with our own things, though not before a lot of amateur carpentry and hand stitching of curtains and so on had taken up a lot of our time.

NO ELECTRICITY

There is no electricity or running water at the top of our hill. Many people in the Administration are beginning to have diesel plants installed, but we use paraffin lamps. They give quite a good light and the whitewashed walls certainly help. This means, of course, that every day before 5.30pm the lamps have to be filled and put in preparation for the sudden advent of darkness, the change from day to night often taking only 20 minutes. Fortunately the house is all on the level so that if you have to walk through with a torch in the darkness you are not likely to fall over anything worse than a cat or land crab. We had a land crab in our bedroom the other night, but fortunately before we went to bed. We heard a lot of scuttling and on investigating saw this monster, with a body like an elongated saucer. He was soon persuaded, with a stick, to continue his moonlit walk outside.

WATER

The water situation does get to be a bit of a problem. There is piped water down in the main village, but as yet, we have not the machinery for pumping it up the hill to us and to many other people. So we rely on tanks; one of them must hold about 800 gallons and the other 400 gallons. This would be all right if there was a constant rain supply, but during the months of July, August and September, only a trace of rain falls, so we will have to be very careful: washing down to the minimum, the cistern pulled only when vital, the half-a-dozen odd cups of tea substituted with oranges, the temptation to wash hands over the running tap over the sink must be shunned, and every drop of rain collected in odd buckets which must then be safely removed from the exploratory hands of Marcus.

Water Tank

Typical Lavatory

Typical Bathroom

OTHER CHURCHES

The other Europeans consist of a Resident Agent, two Agricultural Officers – one Dutch, the other Swiss, both married – a Chief Clerk, an Organising Teacher, two Mormon Missionaries from America, one Shop Owner, a Roman Catholic Priest from Holland, and a Social Worker for a Women's Project, sponsored by America, the only other European woman. You can see what a small, strangely international community we are, and how important it is not to get on each other's nerves. But on this one little island we have four denominations, ourselves (L.M.S.), the Roman Catholics, the Seventh Day Adventists, and the L.D.S. (Mormons).

OUR OWN PECULIAR CHURCH

Many of the church ways here are still relics from Victorian English Christianity: dances are frowned upon, socials are practically non-existent, hats must be worn, and the Missionary must sit in his special pew almost under the pulpit, from where he can only see the Pastor by cricking his neck. The church itself in Arutanga is the most peculiar shape ever seen: its pulpit is situated in the middle of one of the long walls of the building, facing the other long wall, so that the preacher has  a congregation on three sides of him, with the greater number to his left and right. But the people love their services, some of them attending church as many as six times a Sunday: 5.30am Morning Prayer, 8.30am Sunday School; 9.30am Morning Service; 2pm Sunday School (again!); 3pm Afternoon Service, 6pm Bible Meeting. The approach to worship, though, is entirely different from that found in an English Church; there seems to be continuous noise generated mostly by the Sunday School children who are expected to stay in to the whole of the morning and afternoon services as well as their own, and by people reading in stage whispers with the Pastor when he reads the Lessons.

LITTLE TO READ

Of course, there is little here, apart from the Bible, for them to read in their own language. Mr. Thorogood has written some pamphlet booklets for them, and there are one or two other books written by past missionaries, but when we know how desperate we feel when short of ordinary fictional reading matter, we can see what a lot of life is not yet opened up to the Maori people. We do have a daily Press, rather crudely typed and pinned on the notice board outside the post office, which occasionally contains a little world news – our wireless also helps us to keep in touch with many happenings and events, but without these would be completely lost. As soon as the TEAL plane discontinues its run then mail will be our greatest longed for event, for this will be brought once a month on the ship to Rarotonga, though we shall then have to wait still longer for a schooner to bring it over to Aitutaki.

TRANSPORT

Transport also becomes something of a problem at times. There are, of course, no public transport vehicles at all. The villages are scattered (they are set across the island in the shape of a triangle, the three main points being separated from each other by a total distance of about 12 miles) and journeys to any of them are taken along rough sandy tracks. You can travel by bicycle, by horse, by hitch-hiking on a truck or Administration Land Rover, or by hiring a shop truck! There is a TEAL flying boat which comes to our airport once a fortnight, although this flight may stop altogether in October. The Airport is at the extreme northern end of the island, about six miles from us at Arutanga, so we do not have much contact with the few Europeans there.

WE WOULDN'T CHANGE OUR LOT

But, in spite of all this, we are immensely happy here doing this sort of work, and wouldn't change our lot with any one. Christianity has been in the Cook Islands just over 140 years, and our situations can be little different from those about which Paul wrote in his Letters. Indeed with all our problems, both moral and spiritual, we must compare quite favourably with the first 140 years of Christianity. We find it hard not to want to straight away impose the whole of the highly organised English Church life on these people, but that must not come yet.

It is a lovely moonlit night, and looking from this room we can see the grey sea streaked by the light from the moon, the palm trees in our front garden just moving with the breeze; we can hear the sound of a guitar and some singing, intermingled with shrieks of laughter from the local dance hall and cinema show; the crickets also are singing, and now and again a goat bleats; such are the night sounds in our desert island. We must blow the lamps out, pull down the mosquito netting and go to bed, knowing that the sun that bids us rest is waking you all.

LETTERS FROM JUNE 1960 – SETTLING IN NICELY!

HIGHER COSTS IN AITUTAKI
Everything is very expensive here, because the cost of freight from Rarotonga is added on to most goods. This makes one dreadfully careful about wastage. You ought to see me taking rusty bent nails out of packing cases for future use! Most of the constructional jobs about the house are nearly finished although at some future time I want to try my hand at some cupboards and corner wardrobes for the bedroom.

LANGUAGE DIFFICULTIES
At the moment I must get down to serious language study. This presents a problem because each island has many different words for different things. The Bible is in Rarotongan and all preaching is done in that language. If I learn Rarotonga, though, the Aitutaki people will be put out because I don't have the language of my home island.

NEW WATER TANK SOON FILLED
Our water tank is installed now, and fitted up to the sink tap, so we have running water! The day the tank arrived – a 400-gallon one – I casually put the roof guttering pipe over it. This morning the tank was full – all from about ten feet of guttering in the roof! Mind, that was a bit exceptional. It certainly can rain here. I woke at 5am to hear it pouring down, plus thunder and lightning. It woke Marcus also, but not Rita – until Marcus climbed into bed with us.

MAKING A BATH
Tomorrow the church folk are coming along to make us a cement bath. We've done the measuring for it by simply lying down on the floor where it's going and seeing if bottom and elbows will fit inside mysterious chalk marks. We've had to make it small on the principle that the smaller the bath the less water you need to be able to squeeze it high up the sides! Well, it makes sense to me, anyhow!

MARCUS

Marcus is loving his new home here. It took him no time to make friends with everyone and I'm sure that, after only about six weeks, the whole Island knows him. They are of course thrilled that he speaks Maori so fluently and with such a good accent. Sometimes I try a little Maori on him and he looks at me as if I'm mad and then laughs, so I don't get much help from that quarter. He's coming on nicely with English too, and knows that we speak to him in a different language.

COOK ISLAND LEGENDS

I'm having a three-hour language session each week now and at last beginning to see some daylight, though some of the time is spent on a lot of incidentals. The teacher is old and likes to reminisce, and sometimes comes out with wonderful old legends and tales. Today I heard for the first time that the Mission House has been built over an old sacrificial ground, where not only fish and turtles were sacrificed, but also humans. It's quite put Rita off digging in the garden! I have also learnt that the real name of this place is Utataka (corrupted by the Europeans into Aitutaki) which means the place where a man sighted land.

Ru, the first man to land here, so the legend goes, brought sixteen women with him, of whom he took four to be his wives. The second man to come took the rest of the women off to the other side of the island, settling them in various locations, now villages, the names of which have special meanings. For example, the village of Reureu (Ray'oo-ray'oo) – a "suburb" of Arutanga, which means "grey" in English, got its name because the man who first found it had to hack his way through dense bush to reach it. Branches cut across his face, climbers trailed round his neck, and cobwebs got into his eyes so that everything looked misty or "grey".

These old tales are fascinating and I've often told people that they ought to write them all down for the benefit of future generations. On the weekly wireless programme now extended to two hours, they are having Cook Island legends told, in Maori, by the chief speaker of Rarotonga – a deacon of the church – and this is wonderful for the people. I shall have to see if I can make any translations of them.

MARCUS

He still gets as dirty as ever, every time we go to collect him for a meal he looks as if he's been under the tap, rolled in the sand, played with the mud, eaten the chicken food, been in a fight, run through a hedge, and fallen out of a tree. Nine times out of ten that's exactly what he has done. The other day Rita suddenly found him running down the verandah chasing the boy from next door, waving a burning brand out of the stove!

He saw his first pig killed the other day and didn't turn a hair. We're now waiting for the pastor to come in and tell us that Marcus has killed another for him without being asked!

NIGHT SCENE

It's a lovely night tonight. Quite cool again, after a hot day in which the mosquitoes and wasps have been swarming all over the place. From my study window I can see all the lights out in the lagoon – lights from the little fishing canoes. People often go out to fish at night with their lanterns – it's easier to get the fish attracted by the light and fall into the boat, than have to spear them!

Large crickets now and again come sailing across the room, attracted by my lantern. Some are at least three inches long and beat about all over the place. Fortunately there aren't any cockroaches here, or ants. We asked for the house to be sprayed before we came and this has kept them all out. Millipedes still wander into the house but they are a harmless nuisance. I've not seen a scorpion yet, though they are supposed to be about. Cats wander in and out of the house from the pastor next door. They keep the rats away of course but they also give one a nasty fright occasionally. The other night we were sitting peacefully in the sitting room when there came an awful eerie noise of squalling – sounded like the dead spirits of past sacrifices!

We have also had a chicken and her brood in the dining room rummaging round for dropped scraps. So we still have very much the farmyard life out here. On some mornings we may be woken by a bell on our verandah being rung for Morning Prayer, or by some cock who has mistaken the moon for the sun and got up to start his day's work at about 3am!

The moon is certainly bright sometimes. You never see it like this in England – you could almost find a pin dropped in the grass by its light.

LETTERS FROM JULY 1960 – WORK IS UNDERWAY

BIRTHDAY CELEBRATIONS

Many thanks for your birthday telegram which arrived here in the early evening. It made me feel again to be part of the big family birthday celebrations. Rita had planned some marvellous surprises. In the dining room, as I went in for breakfast, I saw strands of wool stretching from all parts of the room and even out of the windows; and at their ends were all manner of presents.

Rita had prepared some great meals. We had strawberries and cream and a glorious birthday cake with candles. In the evening we sat and played Mah-jong, rounding off a wonderful day. Of course Marcus had a whale of a time too. We gave him a matchbox car, but he was far more interested in my presents. He's still full of beans and as lively as anything.

MID-WINTER

Though we are now in the depths of winter, it's a lovely day again today and seems to be getting hotter. However the evenings have been cold enough for pullovers. Our new stove has just arrived and is being fitted today. It has a hot-water tank as well, so we're feeling very modernised.

GARDENING

We have had great fun recently in the garden. The front lawn is a vast expanse divided into two by a path leading up to the house. One half is bare of all trees and the other has a large flamboyant right in the middle. We're trying to turn this half into a private garden by hedging it round with a hibiscus hedge. Rita has spent the last two days planting hibiscus cuttings and having a go at the little strip of garden just below the verandah. We bought some seeds in Rarotonga – pinks, marigolds, asters, etc. Previously this bit of garden was filled with large bushes of hibiscus which not only cut out the light from many of the rooms, but spread their roots in such a way as to be a danger to the verandah wall. So they have been uprooted, after a terrific struggle.

WORK
Work is going very well and there is plenty to do. I'm having discussion-studies and lectures with the pastors, and a discussion-group of church members on set questions for our Church Assembly in October. Also, of course, language lessons.

STARTING A SCHOOL
We have also been busy lately in getting a school started! When Bernard was here he ran a school of higher education for pupils who had left school and yet had not been ready for the Secondary School in Rarotonga. The people here asked if I would do the same, to which I agreed. About 24 children took a simple entrance exam the other day; 18 of them passed this, and we start the school on Monday. The subjects we are taking are Maths, English Grammar and Literature, Geography, History, Law, Woodwork, Current Affairs, Religion. Rita is taking Customs of Europeans, Reading and Cookery. We are also having outside lecturers on Agriculture, Health, and Cook Island Legends. The School will run from Monday to Friday and from 8.15am to 12pm each day. So we shall be really tied up for a bit!

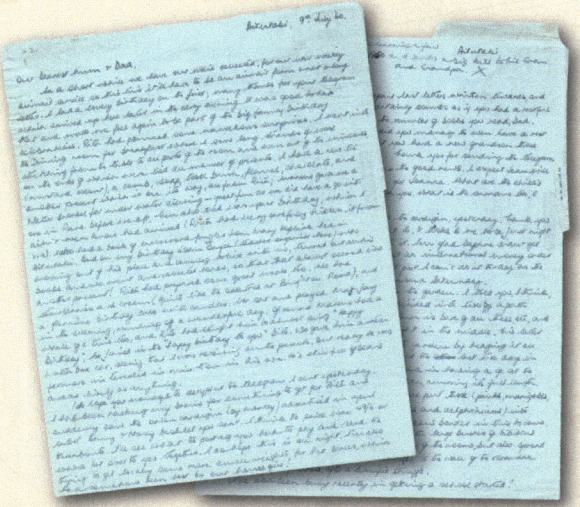

School Classrooms

LETTERS FROM AUGUST 1960 – ISLAND EVENTS

BABY SHOW
Today it is very windy and overcast; we hope this means rain when the wind drops. Our kitchen tank is empty and our bathroom one is only a quarter full, so we are having to be somewhat mean with it. On Friday it is the Island baby show, for which I am one of the judges. I shall probably be unpopular with some of the mums for a day or two afterwards! The local clinic wanted me to enter Marcus but I refused; there might have been some danger of his taking a prize merely for being a European.

STARTING A SCHOOL
Things are getting very busy here now. Most of my time is taken up with this new school. I have 16 pupils whose ages range from 16 to 23 years. Can you imagine me trying to teach percentages and decimals?

YOUTH CLUBS
I've also made some suggestions for starting Youth Clubs in the churches. At present the pastors can't quite reconcile themselves with dancing in any club, so we've got to try and plan without that, although, as all young people here love dancing, we've got to come to it eventually or else lose them.

OLD-FASHIONED SUNDAY SCHOOLS
Rita and I are going to try soon to have a go at grading some of the Sunday Schools, and introducing real Sunday School teaching. We're still rather in the Victorian era of Sunday Schools, in which most of the time is spent in singing hymns and listening to a Bible story. All the children meet together in one large group so you can imagine the sort of bedlam that ensues.

AN ENGLISH SERVICE
I've also started an English service twice a month. At the first we had five Europeans, rwo Maori wives of Europeans and a Maori choir of four sopranos, two altos, two tenors and four basses. Can't have any more because room is limited.

LETTERS FROM SEPTEMBER 1960 – MAKING PLANS

THE COMING "JOHN WILLIAMS" TOUR

We have Bernard staying with us for a few days. He came over for "consultations" (sounds good doesn't it) about our Assembly in October. It really has been good to see him again and to have a proper get together. Plans are going well. Here's a rough itinerary. We board on October 23 and go to Atiu, Mitiaro, Mauke, Rarotonga and then Mangaia, picking up delegates for the Assembly which lasts about five days. The ship then goes to Mauke, where Rita and I are dropped for ten days' solid work with the two churches there. Then we are picked up again and taken to Mitiaro, Atiu, Penrhyn, Manihiki, Rakahanga, Pukapuka and Palmerston. We stay about 36 hours in most of the islands. Then back to Aitutaki. It's a bit rushed but at least we shall have the chance to see all the islands and spend a little time with the people.

RAIN WANTED

It is still hot and dry; temperature in the 80s and rainfall down to about an inch a month. I expect our water tank will last for another ten days and then we'll be making journeys down the hill to the village well.

PONY BUT NO TRAP

We've just discovered the ideal mode of Aitutaki transport – pony and trap. There are hundreds of horses here but no traps. What a boost for the L.M.S. to see the missionary and wife jogging round, with their sunshades up, in the genuine article!

DOUBT ABOUT AIRMAIL
I want to get this letter off tomorrow morning as this may possibly be the last air-mail from Aitutaki. Of course we shan't know until it actually happens – most news here is proved valuable and true or worthless and false by trial and error. We do know that our fortnightly seaplane has stopped. This may be simply a "flash in the pan" flight or the beginning of a new era. If not, our mail in future will have to go on our monthly ship to New Zealand before starting its journey home. So don't be worried if you don't hear from us regularly.

A NEW SHIP
Have you heard about our new ship? The poor old Maui Pomare – from N.Z. once a month – has just about finished its days and has been replaced by the Moana Roa (Long Ocean) recently built in Glasgow. She should be at Curacao now on her way out and should be up to the Cooks about once every three weeks.

MODERNISING THE SUNDAY SCHOOL
I had better explain about our new Sunday School work. I spoke to the pastors about organising them into departments and they seemed very enthusiastic. So we called a meeting of the teachers and are trying to give them a training course. They have cottoned on to most of the ideas very well, except that of expression work, which we are having to ignore for the moment. It's too much like working on a Sunday. However we shall be pleased if all we can do is to separate the age groups one from another. Rita is going to keep a friendly eye on the Arutanga Beginners and Primary; and I have agreed to take the Senior Group (about 20 children between the ages of 16 and 21) who I am hoping will quickly turn into teachers.

THUNDER AND LIGHTNING
We had a terrific thunderstorm yesterday, heralding some desperately needed rain. It took Marcus a long time to get used to the thunder, although he thought the lightning was wonderful. It is good out here not just a flash, but a brilliant electric blue light over the whole sky, sometimes lasting almost three or four seconds.

LETTERS FROM OCTOBER 1960 – THE "JOHN WILLIAMS" TOUR

PREPARING FOR "JOHN WILLIAMS" TOUR

School has finished now and we are spending a frantic fortnight preparing for the arrival of the "John Williams". There are sermons to write, and translate; Boys' Brigade syllabuses to prepare for potted courses; Sunday School Syllabus for our own Sunday School here while we are away; catechism to prepare in 12 monthly parts for inclusion in our magazine; and of course Rita has all the packing to do.

THE ITINERARY

During the actual Assembly at Mangaia, lasting five days, Rita will go to Rarotonga with Jannette instead of them both hanging about in Mangaia with little to do or see. It will also enable Rita to do some Christmas shopping – hopeless in Aitutaki.

They say that today's plane is really the last! We shall believe it when we find that no plane comes in a fortnight's time.

Here is the finalised itinerary of our trip:

Oct 24 – Aitutaki
Oct 25 – Atiu, Mitiaro, Mauke
Oct 26 – Mangaia
Oct 27-Nov 2 – Assembly on Mangaia
Nov 3 – 16 – Mauke
Nov 16 – Mitiaro
Nov 18 – Atiu
Nov 24 – Penrhyn
Nov 27 – Manihiki
Nov 30 – Rakahanga
Dec 4 – Pukapuka
Dec 8 – Palmerston
Dec 9 – Aitutaki

LETTERS FROM NOVEMBER 1960 – THE JOHN WILLIAMS TOUR AND SOME EXCITING NEWS

L.M.S. FOREIGN SECRETARY MEETS JOHN AND RITA

These few days on the John Williams with fortunately fine weather are giving me a chance to catch up a bit with correspondence, and I thought I would like to send a note to let you know that I found John, Rita, and Marcus, well and happy and clearly admirably settled in to the life and work in the Cook Islands.

Unfortunately shipping arrangements did not allow of my going to Aitutaki to visit John and Rita in their home. I should very much like to have done that, though I have a clear recollection of Aitutaki, their house, and the churches, and talking with John and Rita made it all come very much alive for me again. John was, of course, at Mangaia for the meetings of the Church Assembly, and I think must have been encouraged at the general level of the discussions and the decisions that were taken. There is much to be very thankful for. As I compared what was happening with the Assembly in Penrhyn in 1952 the progress was very marked. One of the good features of the situation is the comparative youth of the pastors, with one or two who are really bright and have considerable gifts of leadership. These provide some good colleagues for Bernard Thorogood and John to work with and there is a real readiness to receive the help that they can give – much more so than in some of the other Pacific churches. John preached a good sermon on the Sunday afternoon of the Assembly.

We finally left John and Rita and Marcus at Mauke where they are spending a fortnight helping the two pastors and churches there. When the John Williams gets back into the Cooks in a week's time they will set out on a round of the islands. This will give John his first real chance to get a comprehensive picture of the churches and to see what can be done for them individually. When he has made this on-the-spot contact he will be able to follow up a very worthwhile ministry of encouragement of the pastors by correspondence and occasional visits. I am glad that Rita is able to make this round with him – if they have good weather, as I hope they will, it can be very pleasant.

But this is just a note to share with you the joy I had in this time with John and his family.

Yours sincerely,

C. STUART CRAIG

SOME EXCITING NEWS FROM RITA

Yesterday morning I saw the European doctor and they confirmed that I am pregnant much to my delight and the approximate due date is May 11th. I wired John immediately and had a reply this morning, he is thrilled too. I doubt it will be very long before the news is spread throughout the Cook Islands.

CONFERENCE AT MANGAIA

The Conference at Mangaia was very good. There were about 60 delegates and pastors present and we met in assembly for four days. The final occasion was when the delegates and pastors, on the last evening, presented some items of entertainment for us in the packing shed. One retiring pastor had us in fits when he appeared not only dressed as a woman but also with a high falsetto voice to match. We all agreed that if he put as much into his preaching as into that sketch he would have had a terrific church by now.

COOK ISLAND MISSIONARY FROM PAPUA

We did some serious business and made not only some surprisingly courageous decisions, such as sending unmarried students to Takamoa, but also some far-reaching ones, such as agreeing in principle to sending a Cook Island missionary to Papua. These things mean that the Church out here is beginning to break away from the shackles of past tradition and to stretch forward to higher ideals and greater hopes for the future.

I was of course sorry when I had to say farewell to Bernard and Stuart because I'm sure the fellowship did us all good. On the other hand it was lovely to see Rita back again after her stay in Rarotonga. She appears to have had just as good a time with Jannette there.

AT MAUKE

After leaving Mangaia we came overnight to Mauke where we've been staying for two weeks. We stayed first in the village of Oiretumu with Toka and Tupima, with a student and wife from Takamoa. We have had a frantically busy time but it has all been very well worthwhile. Every night we had a meeting with Deacons, Boys' Brigade Parade, Boys' Brigade Officers, Church Members, and Sunday School Teachers. We have also managed to start a mixed Youth Club. There are only two churches on Mauke so most of these meetings were joining church efforts. By repeating them at the second church, at Kimiangatau, we managed two meetings with each group.

EXPLORING CAVES

Of course we've not spent all our time in meetings. One day we went for a picnic to the sea, with all the church women. Another day we explored some caves, of which there are many on the island. On one occasion we went down through a hole in the earth to a cave underneath. After scrambling for about 15 minutes through the bush and over sharp coral rock we found the narrow entrance down which we had to scramble. Lamps were lit and torches switched on while we crawled, sometimes on hands and knees, below low-hanging stalactites and over sharp rock.

> Then we had to wade, clothes and all through waist-deep water, and finally left a message in a bottle down in the inmost recesses.

This was the first time many of the local people had been down into this cave. I was about the third European man, Rita the second European lady, and Marcus the first European child to go down.

GIFT FROM AN OLD ARIKI

We visited an old Ariki (chief), a Roman Catholic, who showed us all his relics, including stone adzes, human bones, spears, and hundreds of other old Maori tools and instruments. He had some large wooden crochet hooks made years before the coming of the first European. He insisted on giving us a stone plane made and used many years ago. We had to take it for fear of offending him, but it seemed a shame. He insisted so much because one of his ancestors came from Liverpool, where Rita was born.

OFF TO MITIARO, ATIU AND PENRHYN

Now we're waiting for the John Williams to take us on to Mitiaro, four hours away, where we will stay one night. Then we go to Atui, again only four hours away, for one night, and then the long drag up to Penrhyn, leaving Atui on Monday and arriving at Penrhyn on Friday.

MARCUS

Marcus is of course a bit bewildered by so much coming and going and so many people handling him. But it's good in one respect; he has been with us a lot more and so is learning English fast at last. He wakes up at the crack of dawn and often batters at Pa and Ma till they take some notice. And here we are, longing for him to have a brother or sister – how crazy can you get!

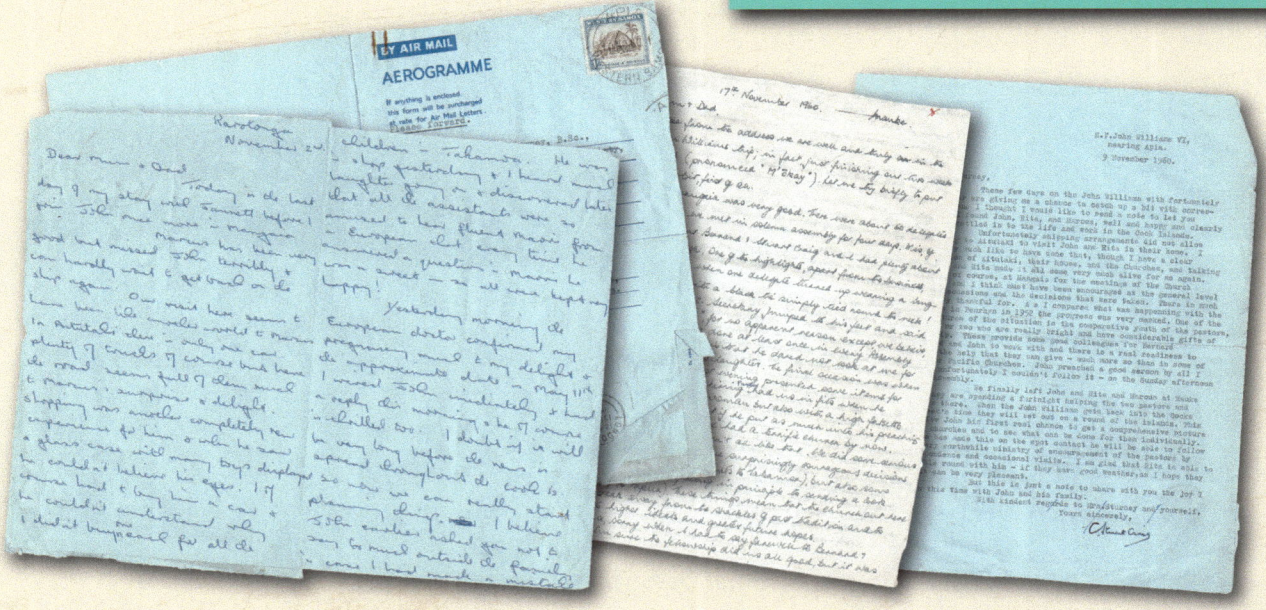

LETTERS FROM DECEMBER 1960 – THE JOHN WILLIAMS TOUR SUMMARY

MAUKE

I promised to record for you some of our experiences of the John Williams trip. It's difficult to know where to start and where to finish. I believe we last wrote to you from Mauke, where we stayed for two weeks. We had a wonderful time there and we shall always remember our stay in Mauke with great happiness. The people were very excited to have us there, even for such a short time. I think one of the greatest experiences we shall remember is travelling down from one village to another. We had a little old Ford truck and they decked it out with paper "eis" and bits of crepe paper all over the place, and flowers; and in the back they put a large mat and two wooden armchairs and we had to sit down on these rather like a King and Queen. The people piled into two big trucks behind us and followed all the way, singing at the tops of their voices. We drove straight into the village there, right through the football field, in between the goal posts, and eventually into the churchyard, where the Mission House is. We even drove up the path leading to the house, so that we were deposited right at the front door. There, about four or five women came round to us, after they had sung hymns and songs, and lifted up the mat on which our chairs were and carried us bodily, mat, chairs and all, into the Mission House.

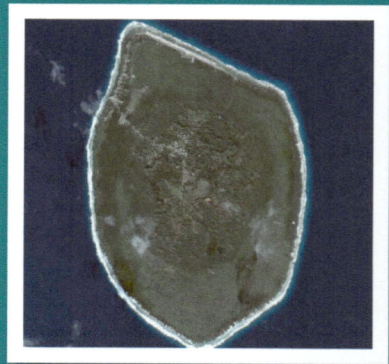

ATIU

Eventually the time came for us to leave Mauke and we got on to the John Williams again and went north, straight to Atiu, about four hours' journey away. Atiu had a man there who had been in a Boys' Brigade Camp at Eton and he had everything very highly organised for us. We had a very nice time there but we didn't get to see the people quite as much as at some of the other islands. We were, what shall I say, segregated a bit more. We of the missionary party were put into the Mission House for eating, while the rest of the people ate in the Sunday School room.

MITIARO

Mitiero is only about four hours by sea from Mauke. We had a most glorious welcome there. We landed in a little cape and came right up over the reef to a place about 50 yards from the shore. There we were supposed to get out and paddle. The church, however, didn't fancy the missionary and his wife paddling, so they had produced a church pew with two enormous poles along underneath it. We stepped straight out of our canoe onto the church pew, sat down on this, and were lifted high in the air by four men at the poles and carried to the shore, up a steep slope in the sand and then quite a long walk right up to the Mission House. You can imagine what they were like at the end of that journey? I think it would have been enough just to carry a church pew! Curiously enough, a similar thing happened to us in Pukapuka. We walked half a mile from the shore towards the Mission House and at the entrance they had a lovely wooden settee all decked out gaily, with poles underneath it, and this we had to sit on and be carried up the few yards to the house, where, in the boiling sun, they had a welcome for us. Most of the welcomes are very much the same. You have to sit down, first of all. The Boys' Brigade and Girl Guides who made a guard of honour for us sing a hymn; we have a prayer, and then usually I have to make a little speech of thanks and greetings to them.

PENRHYN

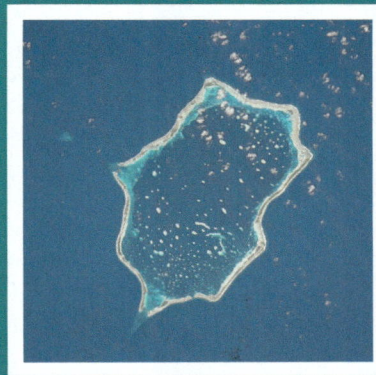

After our 24-hour stay in Atiu we went north to Penrhyn. We had some bad sea on the way up and a very rough trip, with the ship rolling and pitching even though she's a very steady ship and a very comfortable one to travel in. On arrival we had a good welcome there in the Mission House. We went over to the other little village (Tautua) eight miles across the lagoon and visited them for the whole day, having a very pleasant time with them. We looked at their lovely church, made about 50 years ago. It is, surprisingly, quite a dark church, with a lot of beautiful wooden carvings in it. On the outside is a great pencil mark, where once they caught a great turtle, put it up against the wall and drew round it. I should think the diameter of the shell must be seven or eight feet – an enormous great thing.

CATCHING SHARKS

We came back to the main village – Omoka – and went to the services there on Sunday. I had to induct a new pastor into the church there. On Sunday night we went out to catch sharks; we stood on the edge of the verandah wall, right against the sea, threw the baited line over, and hauled up a couple of sharks. I got one and Rita the other. We threw them back in again after we'd had a look at them. We got back to the John Williams again in the morning and left then, to go over to Manihiki.

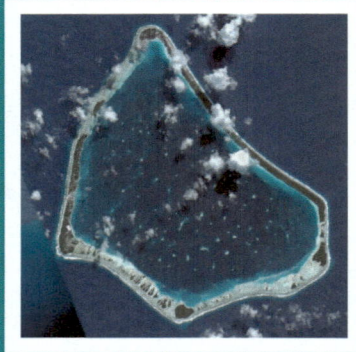

MANIHIKI

We arrived in the main village of Tauhunu and stayed there for most of the first day. The pastor's wife at Tauhunu is the woman who made the handbag which was presented to Princess Margaret when she christened the John Williams ship, and she has photographs of this rather lovely bag round the room. Then we went over in a little motor-powered launch to the other village of Manihiki, across the lagoon, the village of Tukao. We had a very happy time here. We got to know them as much as we possibly could in a short time. At all these islands I had to have Deacons' meetings and try to explain a little bit about the Assembly while Rita went to talk not only to the women but also to the Girl Guides and see how things were going with them.

RAKAHANGA

We didn't stay in Manihiki long as we had to go on to Rakahanga about four hours' north of Manihiki. This is a delightful little island except for the flies, the whole place was absolutely covered in flies. The streets there look as if they have been made into a proper little village with walls along the roads. We had a lovely time there. After my usual Deacons' Meeting we had an uapou as at all the islands and then we went on to see some dancing. These islanders had practised some beautiful dancing for us. I should think they went on solidly for at least an hour without a break. The church there is a lovely church too. Right in the middle of the ceiling there's an enormous great Union Jack, rather an extraordinary thing to see in a church but somehow it doesn't look too out of place.

PUKAPUKA

Then we went on from Rakahanga to Pukapuka. Pukapuka is very much off the beaten track and they have only perhaps two or three ships a year. You can understand how happy they were to see the John Williams come round to them. We landed there in little whaleboats and rowing boats, although we wanted to land in a lovely canoe that they had all decked out for us. However they wouldn't let us get into it because it was full of water. We spent a very nice day in Pukapuka. It is an island very much known for its mosquitoes but we were lucky and saw very few. We had a happy time walking around amongst the people. The food was all put out on a long table – bits of chicken, raw fish, cooked fish as well, heads, eyes and everything lying on the table. We didn't have a great deal to do on Pukapuka because Ta Upu had been there only a short while before us.

PALMERSTON – THE ONE-FAMILY ISLAND

From Pukapuka we went on for a three-day voyage to Palmerston. That's the island which is peopled by the Marsters family. The original Marsters ran away to sea from Gloucestershire, and he landed on this little uninhabited island, found for himself from somewhere three wives and completely peopled the island. There are at present about 99 inhabitants and they all speak English, using quite a lot of old nautical terms and most of them speak with what I suppose must be a Gloucester accent. We were only able to stay for two hours, but just enough time for a few of us to get off and have a look at the island and see just what it was that had attracted the original Marsters. We saw the house which he built and it really is an amazing piece of work. There are four great beams at the corners of the room. They must be at least 18-inches square. These support the roof and go right down into the floor at least three or four feet. Supporting the house underneath, lying horizontally, are more 18-inch square beams. It's a well-known fact that never has the house blown down although Palmerston has been crippled by hurricanes in the past.

We left Palmerston after meeting most of the 99 inhabitants and set sail for Aitutaki, which we reached two days later. We had, of course, a lovely welcome when we got there, and it really was good to be on dry land again.

THE JOHN WILLIAMS

I want to tell you a little about the John Williams ship itself. It really is a most comfortable ship. We had what is called the State Cabin – two bunks, and a long settee on which Marcus slept. Opposite us is the dining saloon, which has two tables in it. All of us and the European crew ate our meals there, sitting anywhere at the table, and had a very happy time all mixed up together. Upstairs is a sun lounge, with a roof over the top, nice deck chairs to sit in. Down below, on the hatch, is where most of the delegates and pastors would sleep with a large awning to protect them not only from the sun but also from the rain. Forward are a few bunks for crews and a few spare bunks into which some of our senior pastors went. I spent quite a lot of time up on the bridge talking to the captain. One evening we went up to have a look at the radar set which is most useful. It enables the John Williams to pinpoint the islands that they reach after dusk and really we could see the coastal outlines of the island we were approaching very clearly on the radar screen. In fact we saw it when the island was only just visible – just before night had fallen. It showed what a great help radar is to a ship like this, travelling round the islands at night.

THE CHILDREN'S SHIP

The ship has a wonderful crew. The captain is a most friendly person and did everything possible to help us. Everything was entirely up to us – as to where we went, what we did, how long we stayed, and so on. We felt it truly was the Missionary Ship. The people at all the islands were so pleased to see their own ship that had come round to them. They all think of it as "their" ship. A lot of them have talked of it as the Children's Ship – they know that children from all over the world have helped buy this ship for the L.M.S.

John Williams was a British missionary associated with the London Missionary Society who played a significant role in spreading Christianity across the Pacific in the early 19th century. In 1821, he arrived in the Cook Islands, specifically Aitutaki, where he introduced Christianity with the help of Tahitian teachers. His efforts led to the widespread conversion of the islanders and significant cultural changes, including the decline of traditional beliefs and practices.

Williams continued his missionary work across Polynesia, but his story ended tragically in 1839 when he was killed by islanders in the New Hebrides (now Vanuatu). Despite his death, his influence remained strong in the Cook Islands, where Christianity became deeply embedded in society.

MARCUS

Marcus seems the best sailor of us all, we're thinking of letting him do the travelling while we stay at home! He had a wonderful time with the ship's crew – all Gilbertese. Many could speak Maori and with a mixture of Maori and English, Marcus got on well. Many times towards the end of the trip he was missing and we found him thoroughly enjoying himself, sitting with them in the ship's launch up forward, listening to them sing songs and tell stories. His English is much improved and by the time he gets home next year he ought to be able to have an intelligible conversation with you! Mind you, he made friends very quickly in many of the islands; in one or two places he went off after an hour or two to play with all the hordes of village children who gathered round.

ISLAND PROBLEMS

We can't point to one island and say that that was certainly the best that we visited, because of course, so much depended on the amount of time that we had, the sort of people they were, the opportunity of meeting them, and the kind of work to be done. At each island I had a Deacons' Meeting, talking about the Assembly and about problems that were worrying the people.

At each island I tried to talk to the Boys' Brigade officers and in one place had to present some brand-new band instruments. They already had them, by the way; I simply had to hand them over formally!

HOME AGAIN – AND HOT

Now, of course, we're making plans and preparations for Christmas. It is going to be quieter this year; a lot of the Europeans have gone away on furlough to New Zealand. There are just a few up at the airport. The airport is still running, although there are no planes coming in any longer. The ground crew are still there fixing up any planes that happen to come across. It's very, very hot now, so hot that I'm sitting here in my singlet. We're sitting in the dining room, where we've now got a large mat up on one wall which we received on our journey. We had loads of presents of course. On the other wall we're going to put up a paddle, used in canoes here, and on the cupboard behind me where I'm sitting there are lots of gifts. An ancient plane, for instance (which looks rather like a stone adze), lots of shells, a stalagmite which we got out of a cave where we went swimming in Mauke, some crab shells, a lovely piece of rope, dried bananas wrapped up in banana leaves – they stay like that for at least a year.

AITUTAKI CHRISTMAS

Nothing is really made of Christmas until the day is upon us. We have had a Festival of Nine Lessons and Carols this year (four Lessons in Maori and five in English) and we put a hand-made Crib on the Communion Table – as last year, in Rarotonga. I shall be preaching (in Maori) in Arutanga on Christmas Day though we are not going to stay for the whole two-hour service.

AFTER-CHRISTMAS PROSPECT

Now I am thinking about the Boys' Brigade Camp, from January 6th to 16th, the start of school term and about another Easter Conference. And in between I have to fit in not only the usual run of Pastors' discussion and lectures, but also a lot of new correspondence with the islands we have visited.

But I really feel, after this trip, that I now know what sort of work I am supposed to be doing here. Before this it was a bit nebulous. I was trying to visualise situations and problems that I knew nothing about.

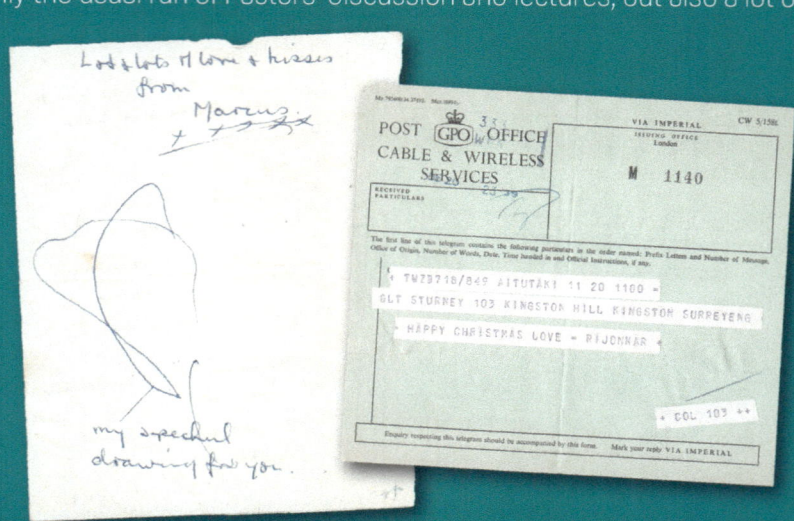

LETTERS FROM JANUARY 1961 – FESTIVITIES UPDATE

A SHIP THAT WENT DOWN
We have to wait such a long time now for letters to reach us. The Moana Roa from N.Z. may come up to Rarotonga once a month with the mail but it sometimes takes an awful long time for a ship to sail over to Aitutaki. That's especially the case now that we are in the hurricane season and we have only one ship tottering about the group. The rest have all shipped off to N.Z. or to Tahiti; or else they have become defunct, as one did the other day, at anchor in Tahiti. Apparently it just sank like a stone.

By the way, it was the ship in which I travelled up north in 1959. I'm not surprised. After that trip I learnt that her bilges were full of loose benzene and it only needed someone to throw a match into them, and we would all have had to swim home!

CHRISTMAS IN RETROSPECT
I had heard that the Christmas Day Service was somewhat of a marathon, lasting anything up to two hours, so we announced to Sam the Pastor that we were afraid we could not stay all that while. After a hectic time opening our presents, and Marcus's as well, we went to the ordinary service, where I preached, telling them the story of the Fourth Wise Man, a good stand by for such an occasion.

Then we made our exit and were taken out to friends at the Airport where, with the Resident Agent and one or two others, we had a very good time. We had as near a Christmas dinner as is possible out here. Rita had done terrific things and it was all a great success. The only things I missed were celery and brussel sprouts. We did have nuts and raisins and mince pies and so on. Most of the afternoon seemed to be spent in washing up!

We stayed there that night and had Boxing Day on the beach, swimming and cavorting most of the day. Doesn't that make you all envious? But we are also a bit envious of your sharp crisp frosts. We stayed out at the Airport on Monday night as well, so felt that we had had a good break. I think it is the only one we shall get this year.

NEW YEAR SERVICES

New Year's Eve came next, of course, and I struggled round to the two outer villages, Tautu (Towootoo) and Vaipae (Wighpie) for their Uapou's. I got back to Rita at about 11.15pm and after midnight had been struck on the official church bell hanging on our front verandah for the whole village to hear, we went down to the Resident Agent.

Sunday New Year's Day was again a real marathon in the church. All the villagers gathered together in Arutanga church for their huge service. There are eight villages and sub-villages in all here. Arutanga and its sub-villages of Nikaupara, Reuteu, Arutanga, Ureia, and Amuri; Tautu; Vaipae and its sub-district of Vaipeka meant sixteen hymns. This all followed the normal 9.30am service. At about 11am Marcus had had enough so Rita took him out. But I went gamely on till 12.45pm – 3 ¼ hours and they hadn't quite finished even then. We spent the afternoon recuperating!

ANNUAL CAMPS

We've not yet started our evening services again partly because there are so few Europeans who would come, and partly to give the choir a break after their magnificent Christmas Carol effort.

On the Monday after New Year's Day we began the annual Week of Prayer, which meant getting up every morning at 5am for the 5.30am service. I made it every morning although I must admit that occasionally I was not completely with the people taking the service.

On the Friday of that week the Boys' Brigade annual Camp started. I had made a lot of the arrangements and programme so felt I ought to be spending quite a bit of the time there. Poor Rita wondered some of the time whether I was coming or going. The Camp, which seems to have been successful, finished last Monday and on the previous Saturday the officers were talking about the Life Boy Camp which always follows immediately after the Boys' Brigade one. Innocently I asked what the programme was, and they told me they thought perhaps I was arranging one as I had done for the Boys' Brigade. So I had to get on with that, and every now and then this week I have to drop in at the Camp to see how things are getting along. So you see life has been its usual hectic round of planning, preparing and visiting.

MARCUS

Marcus's English is getting along nicely now, though most of his words still have to end in a vowel, like Maori ("Picka upa mina cupa", etc.). He's still a monkey, escaping out of the compound just at the time you need him. Sometimes he's playing houses with the family at the back of Sam's (the pastor); sometimes he's down by the well in the village, helping Mrs. Sam to wash the clothes; sometimes he's grubbing about with the family at the back of us; wherever he is, he always comes back dirty. Fortunately he has got used to climbing in under the shower with us now and loves to let the cold water run all over him.

He's also trying to do Maori dances, but only at times when he thinks we can't see him. He doesn't like being laughed at, nor does he like me laughing at Rita or vice versa. If we do, he admonishes us with a stern "no laughing, Mummy!" He's got a terrific imagination and often holds conversations with the air, very serious ones too. He has also taken to bringing us imaginary bits of food, or throwing imaginary fish on Rita's head. Of course we play up and he goes off into hoots of laughter.

He can be very protective at times, too. If Rita is cross with Tai, one of the Sam's boys, he always tries to soften the blow by suggesting giving the boy a sweet. Or as this morning, just as Rita stood up she started coughing and immediately he suggested she got back into bed again because of her cough.

The other night he sang "Twinkle" with Rita giving very little prompting. As he's never attempted to sing it before, we were surprised. I can't say he's frightfully tuneful, though he does enjoy listening to music. Often we find he's switched on the wireless and is curled up in a chair, apparently listening. Goodness knows how much battery he wastes!

LETTERS FROM FEBRUARY 1961 – THE COMING BABY

GIFTS FROM THE COOK ISLANDS

This little parcel is an Anniversary gift, which we thought you'd like. We picked up the shells in the northernmost island of Penrhyn and they really do come out of the sea all polished like these. The mat centre is made from coconut leaves and the fringe from a root vegetable, dyed. The cushion cover, made by the wives at Takamoa, is of the common Cook Island pattern, perhaps the thing most commonly seen in the homes here.

The bananas – first they are dried in the sun for several days, until they are quite brown. Then they are wrapped in dried banana leaves and tied with plaited coconut fibre string. These particular bananas came from Mauke, where they are a speciality. You can eat them at once, if you like, but if left in their wrapping they will keep for up to a year.

The coffee beans are a gift from Mangaia, the island which specialised in pineapples. We have roasted them – and glorious was the smell. After they are picked they are tied in a sugar bag and beaten to loosen the husks. Then comes the long job of separating beans from husks by hand before ordinary roasting in the oven.

THE COMING BABY

In spite of a very hot hurricane season we are all thriving, with only the minor discomfort of prickly heat. We sometimes find it hard to believe that Rita is once again an expectant mother. Our three-monthly plane service is due on March 1st and the Maori doctor is trying to get Rita a seat when it goes to Rarotonga as both he and we feel it a good idea to have a check by a European doctor. This will be Dr. Snowball's first European delivery and I think it will give him more confidence to have a European doctor's confirmation that all is well. Mrs. Withers from the airport, a fully trained nurse with two years' maternity training, and mother of two small children, is coming to stay with us for the birth. It has solved quite a problem for us.

Dr. Snowball (left)

LETTERS FROM MARCH 1961 – AN UPDATE FROM RITA

RITA'S VISIT TO RAROTONGA

I have arrived in Rarotonga and I am now enjoying a lazy evening in the Thorogoods' sitting room. The European doctor is pleased with the way things are going and has told me not to hesitate with plans for having the baby at home. He is doing a day-trip to Aitutaki tomorrow and will let the Maori doctor know that he should have a straightforward case. This I know will put the Maori doctor's mind at rest. It is only a case now of waiting for the baby's arrival and hope that he/she will not make us too anxious by being late.

It was quite a wrench saying goodbye to Marcus. He was rather put out when he first knew about my going away, but when promised a present on my return I think he was rather anxious for me to leave! It should be easy enough to buy what he has asked for 1st choice, a truck; 2nd, a boat; 3rd, a plane. I did my food shopping this afternoon and tomorrow morning I am doing what one might call the pleasure shopping. I only hope I can get it all back on the plane plus half a sack of potatoes.

LETTERS FROM APRIL 1961 – PREPERATIONS FOR THE NEW ARRIVAL

AN EASTER YOUTH CONFERENCE
We have just returned from a hectic Easter weekend conference. It followed the lines of the one we held last year in Rarotonga, though this was much smaller. We decided that the 120 we had last year was rather too many to cope with so we restricted our intake to 50. In fact we finished up with only 32 but in spite of that or perhaps because of that we had a much better conference. We had a high proportion of young school teachers who had come prepared to enjoy themselves in a young adult way. We held the conference in the local school grounds a quarter of a mile from us in sort of camping conditions, though not under canvas. Three women from each of the three Aitutaki churches cooked for us under Rita's supervision, and one man from each church cut the firewood.

We stayed up at the school with them, taking our double mattress, and one for Marcus, and 'camping' properly with the rest. We even joined in their sport on Saturday afternoon – a basketball and softball knock-out competition. Rita refereed the basketball and I played for one of the teams in both games. I'm only just recovering from stiffness after my first bit of exercise for ages.

We introduced the idea of Youth Clubs to the conference, in the hope that some of the young people would take them up. And so today four of them have indicated that they want to start one. I think we've succeeded.

PREPARING FOR THE BABY
Rita is keeping very well but it is awfully tiring for her in this continuing sticky heat. We shall both be very glad not only when the baby comes but also when this hurricane season is over and we begin to get a few cool breezes again. I'm looking forward to a nice crisp frost when we come home! Marcus is also getting well prepared for the baby. We've moved him into a smaller bedroom next to ours. He has been helping Rita to wash all sorts of necessary things – cat net, bed covers, and so on. We are hoping that through all this he'll have quite a soft spot for the baby when it comes. Though we keep saying "it"; many people have tried to foretell the sex. We've been practising Marcus with the proposed names – Sally Christina Mary or Simeon Charles Rodger. He certainly gets on better with "Sally" but yesterday managed "Simeon" as well.

ALL READY FOR THE BABY

We are waiting for the next 20 days to pass quickly. Rita keeps very well in spite of having to endure the hottest months of the hottest hurricane season for some years. Officially we're out of the season now and should be approaching our slightly cooler winter, but we still toss and turn at night in temperatures high in the 70s.

The new baby's room is all prepared, baby clothes in the airing cupboard, pram and carri-cot scrubbed, a mosquito net made for the cot, and clothes being made thick and fast. Dr. Snowball has said that he wants to be called as soon as pain starts – his first European baby! – and Janet Withers is moving in the minute things begin to happen. It's like planning some military operation. The Resident Agent is ready to be called any time of day or night in order to send out the truck for Janet. I only hope the baby doesn't arrive on a Friday night for we couldn't get a telegram off to you till Monday morning.

MARCUS

Marcus still gives us the "willies" occasionally with his wandering. He was lost yesterday and we went off into the bush, and along to the people up the road, and down to the wharf, and round the neighbours (who all think we're daft in our concern for one small boy) but he turned up of his own accord just as we were going to get the Guides out to do some practical tracking. His English is still a bit limited and we could only get out the fact that he had been to see the "caterpillar", by which he means the tractor. Thank goodness we're not in Africa with snakes and lions!

A VERANDAH SUN PARLOUR

I have just finished making an airing cupboard round our hot water tank and yesterday I started to block in one end of the verandah with lattice work, made from the long roots of the pandanas tree. Each root is split into four parts to make thin slats, and they make a good substitute for trellis work. I am doing this job to make a little private sun-parlour where we can put Rita's bed during her convalescence, using it afterwards as an afternoon lounge.

School still progresses, as does Sunday School work, giving us not a few headaches. At the moment we are in the throes of starting a Youth Club in Arutanga. Thirty people turned up to our first full discussion about it last week and we plan to open on May 15th.

Letters from May 1961 – Birth under the most challenging circumstances

BIRTH THROES OF A YOUTH CLUB
I am still being kept pretty busy. We finish school this week for about four weeks, which will be a welcome break. Other things go on as usual. Our first Youth Club is in the throes of being born. After the Easter Conference four girls came along and asked if we could start one. We had a long chat, throwing up loads of ideas, looked at Bernard's suggested Constitution for this kind of Church Youth Club, and agreed to have a meeting of all who were interested.

ABOUT THE SUNDAY SCHOOL
My monthly Deacons' and Sunday School Teachers joint meetings are still going strong. This Tuesday all the Deacons from the three villages are coming. I try to split the programme into two halves.

The Sunday School teachers come on Thursday. I'm going to make them look back over the first quarter's work and ask questions about success or failure. Then I think we'll divide them into departmental groups and do some practical activity work with them. The Sunday School at Arutanga with which we at the moment are most concerned, is coming on by leaps and bounds. So far, the Preparation Class is an outing which the teachers look forward to eagerly. We have even persuaded the teachers to sit with their children during the morning service in church.

All of this is a far cry from what we found when we first came and we have to stop every now and then and give little words of praise and notes of encouragement. For instance Rita has just left a note of praise for a Beginners Leader who has come early for the past two weeks to get her room prepared.

DESK STREWN WITH PAPERS
My desk is strewn with papers again – letters needing a reply by this mail; cut-outs from the Chronicle waiting to be stuck into scrap books for future reference; school exam papers for tomorrow's end-of-term exams; the outlines of talks for this week's meetings; the beginning of circular letters to the outer island pastors; books in current and past use; and bills waiting to be paid. I look at all this and resolve to be firm with myself in future!

In the following pages, you will journey through the deeply personal and harrowing experience of John and Rita as they welcomed their son, Simeon, into the world under the most challenging circumstances in the Cook Islands. With limited medical resources and immense uncertainty, their story is one of resilience, love and hope amidst adversity. While these pages offer a glimpse into their ordeal, you'll find John's full account of those life-changing moments – written years later – at the end of the book, offering deeper insights into their extraordinary journey.

16 MAY 61

SIMEON 14 MAY 8 POUNDS BOTH VERY WELL LOVE = JOHN +

18 MAY 61

SIMEON NOT VERY WELL RITA PERFECTLY FIT = JOHN +

20 MAY 61

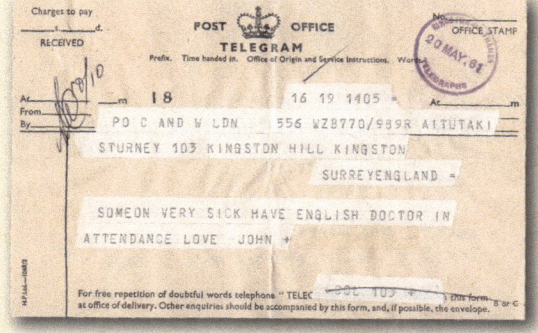

SIMEON VERY SICK HAVE ENGLISH DOCTOR IN ATTENDANCE LOVE JOHN +

23 MAY 61

SIMEON COMPLETELY OUT OF DANGER PROGRESS WONDERFUL +

ANXIOUS DAYS WITH SIMEON

I do hope that you get this letter soon so that we shall relieve your minds of a little of the worry that you must have been going through when we sent our telegrams to you. Let me say right now, though, that at the moment of writing, Simeon is really and truly out of danger, and that he is improving at a tremendous rate. As you know he was born on the Sunday at 4.30pm. Poor Rita had rather a rough time because he was such a long time in coming. But the actual delivery was very quick. The doctor was just preparing to do an episiotomy when all of a sudden the baby was there.

Everything seemed quite normal from then until the Monday night. Simeon was being looked after by Janet Withers (trained nurse, married to an airport man) who had promised to come in and let Rita get a few restful nights before taking over. Suddenly she came to me just as we were preparing for bed and said that she was taking Simeon to the hospital because she was worried about his breathing. She took him down not knowing how she got there in the dark, and she and the doctor fought for two hours for his life. It was then discovered to everyone's horror that there was no oxygen at the hospital. But fortunately the next day we got some from the airport who use it for welding.

A 24-hour watch had to be kept from then and almost continuous oxygen given, but of course the supply was running out! So the Resident Agent, who couldn't have been more helpful, spoke over the radio telephone to Rarotonga asking for a further urgent supply, and for one of the two European doctors to come over. The only available ship was a small yacht newly arrived from New Zealand who agreed to rush over. It left Rarotonga on Wednesday afternoon, and was expected Thursday night, and we only had about 20 more hours of oxygen left. The Resident Agent put on an all-night watch on Thursday night, and a N.Z. naval party (who is surveying in Aitutaki at the moment) agreed to have their launch standing by. But nothing came on Thursday, except one false alarm of the yacht's arrival. Fortunately we had been able to cut down the oxygen, and so still had a little left for real emergencies. On Friday morning the yacht came in to everyone's exhausted relief, and the doctor rushed up here. Just after his arrival Simeon was cut off oxygen altogether and he started to improve. From that time he has gone from better to better.

OUT OF DANGER

The doctor has diagnosed brain damage. He thinks that in the final contraction the baby's head, which had been squeezed so tightly, suddenly expanded at the moment of birth and damaged some tissues in the brain. At the moment it appears to be tissues connected with the breathing only, and he is very hopeful that the reserve tissues are taking over the work of the damaged ones, so that Simeon will suffer from no permanent mental effects at all. Of course, he says it is still early to say, but he is very confident, and very pleased with Simeon's progress; so much so that he is going back to Rarotonga tomorrow without any worries for him. Of course he told us all the things that might happen later, but we, like him, are completely confident that the damage is being repaired itself, and there will be no after effects at all. He wants to see Simeon again in six months time when, he says, he can make a much truer assessment of his real progress. We must just be patient and wait, but he is absolutely out of all danger now, and doing extremely well.

Hospital

MARCUS & SIMEON

Marcus has been a perfect little angel throughout all this worrying time, spending most of his days over with Mrs. Sam next door. Of course he must have known that there has been something wrong though we have tried hard to keep it from him. Now that Rita has the baby on her own he's thrilled. He's as proud as punch over his young brother and takes every opportunity of bringing people in to see him.

He likes to come along at feed or wash time and very gently stroke the baby's face or kiss him: and he was thrilled last night when the baby gripped his finger. Whilst waiting for a feed yesterday Simeon was rather raucous and Marcus ran to get him a toy, the largest plastic car in his playbox! But he only meant Simeon to hold the string on it, and was quite disgusted when he wouldn't. He held him once, like a proud father, but dreadfully worried all the same, and it wasn't long before I was left holding the baby!

A WONDERFUL NURSE

As you can probably see by this letter the sort of changes we have been through. At one time we were almost without any hope left, but Simeon, with his ox-like constitution, just hung on and absolutely refused to give up: and he made us hang on too. And now we just can't stop thanking God for what seems like a miraculous recovery. Everything worked together for good from the very start of the trouble. When Janet rushed Simeon down to the hospital from our house on the Monday night, she didn't know the direction at all. She went charging down our 60 steps, which are anything but sure and firm, with the baby in one arm and a hurricane lamp in the other. She knew vaguely where the doctor lived, and suddenly, without any warning, found herself standing outside his door. She still just doesn't know how she got there and is quite sure she was led by God. Some days, during the crisis, I was very depressed and yet on others I felt as if a huge great burden had been lifted, but that was only after I had completely surrendered everything to God. I knew I couldn't batter against His will, and that I couldn't bargain with Him, nor make promises to Him; I knew I couldn't make God heal him, though at times I prayed very hard; I knew also that this sickness was in no sense of punishment to us, nor was it avoidable in any way. And therefore, the only thing I could do was to surrender completely, and just wait patiently.

I said that this was quite unavoidable. That is perfectly true, and the doctor has reassured us that it could have happened to Rita in Aitutaki, or Rarotonga, or even in London. There is no blame attached to anyone at all, least of all the Maori doctor who has been absolutely perfect. It was he who helped to save Simeon's life on Monday night, and we have only praise for him and Janet, who nearly wore herself out with watching Simeon through every day, and at least half of every night, getting about four hours' sleep most nights.

HELP FROM RESIDENT AGENT

All the people have been very good. The Resident Agent just couldn't have done anything more. He put trucks, telephones, water, everything at our disposal. He was also up at 2am on the night of the expected arrival of the yacht and went down to check that the police watchers he had posted were still at their posts, and the lamps were all filled. He put on every available light to guide the yacht. The Maori people have been wonderful, too, after they heard that Simeon was so ill, bringing us countless gifts: eggs, taro, chickens, beans, etc. Our housegirl, who with her husband stayed with us until 11pm on the night of the expected arrival of the yacht, and all along has been very helpful, brought in a lovely mat this morning as a gift to the new baby. So you can see just how wonderful everyone has been.

RITA

Rita is doing very nicely now, although, of course, everything has been a dreadful strain for her, especially as she was supposed to stay in bed all through the crisis. But naturally she couldn't stay there when so much was going on, and this has all put her back a bit, even though she is up and about now, but having to take everything very easily. She had three stitches after the birth, and with her exertions of the past week has managed to break them all, but the doctor does not seem very worried. She is rather pale, and is going to have a blood count soon just to see if she needs a few iron tablets. She was really wonderful throughout the whole birth (I was with her all the time), and never complained for one moment. And she took all the subsequent troubles extremely well, though I know how she must have been suffering, especially at times when we almost gave up hope. But she is well on the mend now, and very happy.

SIMEON'S PROGRESS

You'll be pleased to hear that things are going on well. Simeon, in spite of all his troubles, is making very good progress, and, of course, we are overjoyed. The more we see of him the more we are sure that the brain damage has only affected his breathing, which the undamaged tissues are coping with extremely well. We get more certain every day that he will have a complete recovery before very long. He has already lost a lot of his breathlessness after the exertion of drinking his milk. And he has lost nearly all traces of bluishness around the eyes and mouth.

MARCUS & SIMEON

Marcus still loves his baby brother. He had the option yesterday of coming to church with me or of staying at home with Rita. He chose the latter with the sweet reason that he wanted to help with his baby Simeon. In actual fact he spent the morning over at the Sams', but nevertheless the thought was there. This morning he led the tribe from next door (the Sams' four children) through the sitting room and bedroom to get to his room. Rita, who was feeding Simeon, said she didn't even hear them until their heads appeared round the bedroom door.

LETTERS FROM JUNE 1961 – A LITTLE UPDATE

MARCUS & SIMEON

Marcus loves Simeon, holds his hands, strokes his hair, smells his face, showers kisses on him, and sings raucous Maori songs right in his ear to help him go to sleep! He is very protective towards Simeon and won't have any of the children from next door making a noise when they come through the house. Of course, it doesn't matter that Marcus shouts at the top of his voice to tell them to be quiet, as long as they all come in on tip-toe. He's even beginning to understand that Simeon can't play with his toys yet, and that he can't eat the solids Marcus likes to present to him from time to time. If they go on like this I think they'll become quite good friends a bit later on. At least Simeon has this advantage over Marcus: he has got a big brother to teach him many of the bad and naughty things of life!

COMING VISIT TO RAROTONGA

I'm afraid that I shall be leaving Rita soon to go over on a quick visit to Rarotonga. Bernard has been away at a Missionary Conference of all Missions in the Pacific, at Samoa. He's just returned so I want to go over for consultations! This is our official District Committee meeting – between just the two of us! Still it will be nice to see Rarotonga again, as I've not been back there since we left a year ago.

The hot weather has now broken and some of the nights are cold enough to put a blanket back on the bed. The rain still falls intermittently, although we should be fast approaching the dry season and with the large tank only half full!

LETTERS FROM JULY 1961 – TUMMY TROUBLE

SIMEON'S TUMMY UPSET
Simeon has a strange tummy upset at the moment, making digestion rather difficult. Dr. Snowball radioed last week to Rarotonga for advice and they suggested that he should be put on the breast again. So now he has two feeding mums! One comes at 6am, 10am and 2pm in the morning and the other at 6pm and 10pm in the evening. The latter has had to sleep at the house several times because Simeon was too tired to wake up for his last feed. The Moana Roa calls here on Friday with Dr. Romans (Chief Medical Officer) on board, so he'll be able to make personal observations. Possibly Simeon may have to go to Rarotonga to be observed by the European staff at the hospital. I'll have to go there in anycase, so we may all go together.

COMING VISIT TO RAROTONGA
My visit to Rarotonga is for our Executive Meetings. They may last only three days but because of waiting for a returning ship I may be away from Aitutaki for two weeks. You can't just hop on a train and come home!

JOHN A SCHOOL TEACHER
I've a new, very temporary job - school teaching. (Not in my own school, which I haven't reformed since Simeon's birth.) I'm teaching Senior English to a group of School Teachers entering for a Government Service examination. They have to pass this in order to get an increase in their salaries.

MARCUS & SIMEON
He gets very worried if Simeon is left to cry too long, caring for him like a mother hen, fussing around, holding his hand, stroking his head very gently, rubbing his face against his cheek and so on. His greatest reward is a smile from Simeon. He's always asking Rita to tell Simeon what he, Marcus, is doing, especially if it's something like building houses with his bricks that we've praised him about.

ON THE MOANA ROA
I am trying to write this on board the Moana Roa, en route to the Executive Committee meetings in Rarotonga. I left on Saturday and we are going via Atiu and Mauke, giving me a good opportunity to renew some acquaintances first made on the John Williams trip last year.

SIMEON'S CHECK OVER
Dr. Romans came on this ship to Aitutaki, gave Simeon a good check over and said there was nothing seriously wrong with him. He believes him to be one of quite a number of children who can't take milk at this age. He still puts on weight which the doctor says is a very good sign. He saw no need for Rita to take Simeon to Rarotonga. Rita and Marcus came out in the launch to see me off and spent ten minutes on the Moana Roa, looking round. I hope Marcus doesn't give his mother too bad a time while I am away.

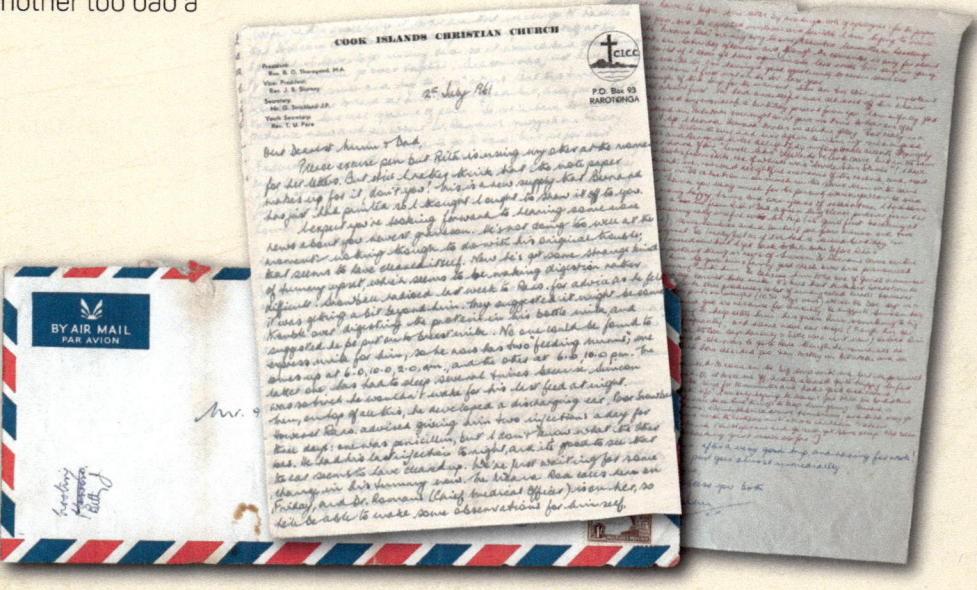

LETTERS FROM AUGUST 1961 – FURTHER HEALTH ISSUES

SIMEON'S HERNIA
Simeon has settled down a bit now but unfortunately it has been discovered that he has a hernia so of course he's getting properly spoilt as we're not supposed to let him cry too much. Rita suspected it about six weeks ago. We'll have to have him operated on towards the end of our furlough, though I'm not sure that it should be done under 18 months. We'll have to see. He gets a little pain from it occasionally, but not continuously, as he used to have with his spasms.

We are definitely home for Christmas. Perhaps five days before. I trust you'll have the red carpet all the way from London Airport!

THE CAR HAS COME
We have a car now, and it's a real delight. Of course it's the property of the Church Council, so we pay for appropriate jaunts. But it is garaged at our house and we use it just when we want to.

AFTER THE EXECUTIVE MEETING
You will have gathered that we have finished our Executive Meetings. I returned to the fold last week, having been away all but three weeks – and Rita looked not the slightest bit harassed. She had even made me a "Welcome Home" cake! The Executive was good. The main outcome for me is that now I have to type out our new hymn book of 400 hymns.

SIMEON
Simeon is leaping ahead now. He has found his fingers to be an amusing source for experimenting, holding them up, clasping them together and finally trying to stuff the whole lot into his mouth. He knows us by looks and voices. If a stranger talks, he doesn't bother to turn his head but if it is one of us, he swings round at once. He smiles, gurgles, and blows bubbles galore. He won't sleep much during the day, but is very happy if propped up against a pillow just high enough to see the world around him.

BERNARD THOROGOOD'S CIRCULAR LETTER

PACIFIC CHURCHES MEET IN SAMOA

This year we have had the joy of the first meeting of churches in the Pacific, at Malua College in Samoa, and although this meant two months separation for us, with Jannette holding the fort here, it was a good beginning. I think most people in this part of the world feel the need for greater fellowship between such isolated churches. In Samoa, where I was a delegate of the Cook Islands Christian Church, along with Ta Upu Pere, we were able to meet folk from Dutch New Guinea in the west to Tahiti in the east – a vast variety of islands and churches. The more we learn about each other the more we see our own weaknesses. For me this meant an eye-opener on the speed of change and the need for the church to allow missionaries to take a back seat. In the Cooks the people are still keen to keep the missionary on a pedestal, and the time is probably here when we shall just have to refuse to accept nomination as President of this and Chairman of that. Perhaps local leadership will not really grow unless we take such a firm line. Samoa was a lovely place to hold a conference and we all enjoyed being waited on by motherly Samoan ladies. We had some disappointments, for example when the Anglican contingent (including five Bishops) failed to accept the invitation to a united communion service (Church of South India), but we should be foolish not to expect such difficulties. We had some really fine speakers, especially the Bishop Lesslie Newbiggin, and made some hopeful moves for the future – the South Pacific now has its own I.M.C. Secretary, a Samoan pastor, who will be a living link between the churches.

THEOLOGICAL MEETING IN FIJI

From Samoa we went on to a further week's talking at Suva, Fiji, on the subject of theological education. There is a real opportunity of lifting standards through all the islands by establishing a Central Theological College in Fiji. It will mean a struggle for us here in Takamoa to lift the standard of our students so that they can enter an advanced course which will all be taken in English. Of course not all our men will be able to go as far as that, but we badly need those with a better educational background. To be able to mix with students from all the other island groups and the other denominations will in itself be an education and will give us men with a far wider outlook.

LIFE IN SAMOA

It is good to have the chance to visit these other islands. Samoa is beautiful, though hotter than Rarotonga, and it has a distinctive native architecture with handsome oval thatched houses. Our first night in American Samoa, where we waited for the little plane to take us over to Western Samoa, was spent in these thatched houses, without walls, around the village square. Life is communal and you need practice to sleep well as the village chatters and laughs its way through the night. They even had a loudspeaker which seemed to be blaring instructions to all and sundry until midnight. But to enter Samoan life in this way was a fine introduction to the conference. Suva is a metropolis, a city of Indians rather than Fijians, thick with little Indian shops; the home port of many inter-island vessels; and the centre of advanced educational work. It is a hot spot sociologically (three races with economic rivalry between them) and a challenge to the church. The Methodists have a big work there and among the Indians there is an exciting evangelistic programme. The airport of Nandi is 60 miles across the island and is now a full-scale international terminal, with air-conditioned lounges and jets roaring off at ghastly hours of the early morning. We were there on a Sunday and were taken to preach at little village churches in the district. My village was called Lomolomo and the surprising thing to me was the careful ritual of kava drinking before and after the service. You sit with the men on the floor in a circle around the large wooden bowl, while a young man squeezes water through the fibre until the juice is all extracted. Then a coconut cup is passed ceremonially and you gulp down the gingery muddy stuff. This is the Pacific way of entertainment and of deliberation. In the Cooks it was dropped many years ago, but it is clearly still a big part of life in Samoa and Fiji. In Suva city, I noticed how the whole thing has become debased, and dirty little kava saloons collect a circle of men on the pavement around a very unhygienic bowl.

SCHOOL CHILDREN'S HOSTEL IN RAROTONGA

Here in Takamoa we are busy on a new project. There is just one secondary school in the Cooks built at Tereora, which is where the L.M.S. school used to be 50 years ago. To this Government school come children from all the islands, with the aim of reaching a School Certificate standard. There are no dormitories, and many of the outer island children are just dumped in households in Rarotonga which cannot afford decent accommodation. We hear of 14 children in a house of two rooms, and so on – no surroundings for doing homework! So the church is building a hostel here in Takamoa to take 40 children, and we hope to have it ready for the school year starting next February. It will mean quite a revolution in our way of life as a college. Hitherto, for a hundred years, the students have each had their own kitchen and looked after their own meals individually. Now it will become communal living, with one kitchen and dining hall where the students and their wives will eat with the school children. The students will act as parents to the children – a responsibility which will give them every opportunity for developing their pastoral talents. We shall be happier knowing that food the students are eating – often they have had a thin time in the past if their families have not been able to finance them properly. So there are two dormitories to go up as well as the dining hall, and the Rarotongan churches are doing the work voluntarily. This means a horde of men descending on the compound, heavyweight foremen clamouring for instant obedience from their subordinates, women admiringly providing a mid-day meal – utter chaos which nevertheless produces quick results. It is like this with any communal effort. When they whitewash the church here (the building, not its members) the young men put up a great scaffolding and swarm over the walls, brushing on the lime wash with bits of coconut husk if they can't find a brush. The big job gets done in a couple of hours. It will be exciting for us to see this work going on in the next five months. Then we shall have the job of selecting the most needy children to come in. Feeding them won't be easy, though there is a government boarding allowance which helps a bit. We shall rely on the churches to send us supplies of taro and coconut, arrowroot and dried fish. The L.M.S. is helping to pay the cost of this scheme and we feel it will be a good sign of the care for children which we preach about.

VISIT OF THE GOVERNOR-GENERAL

Our recent excitement was a visit by the Governor-General of New Zealand. He is Viscount Cobham, and has proved to be an excellent man in the public life of New Zealand, even daring to criticise such a national folly as secularised education, and admired for doing it. He came with his wife and three children on a cruiser and as they were here on a Sunday we had them all at church and then here for morning tea. The church bulged at the seams and many folk sat on pews in the courtyard, so it was a thrill to preach. We are thankful for opportunities like this, when the formality of the occasion itself can serve the Gospel. The party proved very easy to entertain, and the Boys' Brigade and the Girl Guides put on a great show for the Guard of Honour. In politics in New Zealand the great subject for debate at present is, of course, the European Common Market. We hear echoes of the thunder. Most politicians fear the loss of their safe British market for exports, and forecast a considerable drop in the New Zealand standard of living. Should this happen then the islands will feel the pinch also, for the subsidy would certainly be cut. This might not be such a bad thing. It would compel administrators to overhaul their offices and cut out waste. It might also encourage greater local initiative. But there would also be fewer jobs and so some suffering.

The Thorogood Family

KEEN NEW STUDENTS

In the college we are happy about some new students coming along. One came in from Government teaching this year, and another has applied to come next year, leaving the job of radio operator. So men are prepared to give up a relatively well-paid job to enter college, and they are a good deal brighter than average. We pray that in God's good time, and with some pushing by mere missionaries, one or two will reach a degree standard academically, and then we can leave Takamoa in their hands.

LETTER FROM SEPTEMBER 1961 – 10 WEEKS TILL FURLOUGH

DAY SCHOOL DISCONTINUED
It's night time out here – quarter past eight – a still calm night. I can see the lights of a few fishermen out on the lagoon – pressure lamps that they take out for flying fish.

I haven't any school at the present moment. There are a lot of other things that I wanted to do and I had a talk with Bernard Thorogood about it and decided that it would be best to leave the school for the moment.

WORK ON THE NEW HYMN BOOK
Most of my time is being spent on the new hymn book that we hope to have ready by next July or August. It's quite a large job but Ta Upu and Bernard have been through a lot of hymns already and have fitted tunes to most of them. We've written some as well. I've got the job of going through the book, checking up on the tunes to make sure they fit, and typing the whole thing out. There are 360 hymns – 340 Maoris and 20 English – and I've got to finish the job by the end of September so that we can start finding someone to publish it either in England or in Australia. You can imagine that it's rather a big task. We tried, with our tunes, to fit most of the hymns to tunes in Congregational Praise and in Sankeys – people out here love the Sankey tunes. I've noticed a lot of corrections that need to be made. The last time the book was printed nobody checked the proof and there were scores of printing errors.

SIMEON
Simeon is getting along by leaps and bounds. Today, for the first time, we were able to put him out on the verandah in his pram, almost in his birthday suit and he had a good kick in the sun and tried to catch some of the sunbeams. It hasn't really been hot enough for him to do that before but today we almost came into our hurricane weather again though it's not due until October or November.

ONLY TEN WEEKS OR SO!
A lot of our other work of course is packing up and getting ourselves ready to come home. The time here has flown by so quickly and now we realise that we've only another ten weeks or so. We read in the press the other day that there's a plane service direct from Auckland to London. We're wondering whether we might get on to that so that we'd be home within two days of leaving Auckland which would be wonderful.

I'm still doing a bit of work on the house. We have the hot water system installed and we have a pipe running up towards the ceiling in case it boils. It's been boiling such a lot that I've had to take the roof off and fit a new bit of pipe on so that it goes right outside. I'm waiting now to find that I haven't put the roof back straight and that we have a leak!

REBUILDING THE NEXT-DOOR HOUSE
There's a lot of work going on next door in the rebuilding of the pastor's house. Some weeks ago the whole thing was knocked down and they went to live further down in the village. Now all the people of Arutanga have got started on the building. They've cleared all the rubble away and have laid the foundations. Today they started building the walls. They're hoping to finish in about three weeks' time.

It's wonderful to see the work of building that goes on here. Everybody from the village comes up; there must have been at least 50 people up here today and their wives all came up at lunch time bringing their food and they sat on the grass. We took some photos of it so that you can see what a jolly outing it is.

SIMEON'S BAPTISM

A brief resume of last Sunday's events. We ought to tell you first about the Godparents. We had a Godfather and a Godmother. Mr. Thorby was the Godfather: during the time that Simeon was very sick he was so sure that he was going to get better that he said he was going to be Godfather, and just lately he told us that he had already ordered a Christening mug. We hadn't the heart then to tell him that we don't have Godparents and we thought that if he was going to be Godfather we would like Janet Withers, who did so much for us, to be Godmother.

It was a baptism that the church will always remember. We took Simeon down to Thorby's first, to have him dressed, and then into church, Mr. Thorby carrying him. He started crying just after getting into church. Rita volunteered to take him from Mr. Thorby but he said he wasn't going to give in unless Simeon made him. In fact he managed right up until it was time to hand him to John. Simeon looked absolutely adorable – all pink and white, and smelling very beautiful – in fact a model baby. But when he started to cry he looked red and angry and miserable – people in the church won't forget the noise he made!

CHRISTENING PARTY

Rita has made a terrific lot of preparations – cooking etc. for days and days, with a Christening cake and all the falalals. There were 17 people altogether, including us. Unfortunately Mrs. Snowball (doctor's wife) was sick. The only "outsider" was Judge Morgan, a friend of Mr. Thorby. We had Mr. Thorby; Janet; her husband and two children; Sam, of course, and his wife; Snowball, who delivered Simeon; our housegirl and her husband; and two feeding mothers.

I must tell you about the flowers – typical Maori. Half the time there aren't any flowers in church. On Saturday Mr. Thorby gave me some of his prize zinnias and I made the Communion Table an absolute blaze of colour. On the harmonium I made a very subdued show of pale yellow and white zinnias – very delicate and "baby" looking. When we got to church on Sunday, however, we saw that somebody hadn't thought they were arranged well enough and had stuck in a whole lot of white chrysanthemums – miles taller than the things I'd put in – shoved in anywhere.

HOMECOMING DATE FIXED

Definite news at last about our travelling dates. We are booked on the December 6th "Moana Roa" and hope to get a plane around the 16th, arriving home three days later. So we will in fact be home just in time for Christmas. A little bit of a rush for Christmas preparations, but better that way than two or three days late. Marcus is getting very excited about his holiday in "Grandma's Island" but I rather suspect it is because he knows we are arriving at Christmas time, which for him, with his one-track mind, means presents.

MARCUS & SIMEON

In the last post we had a parcel of winter clothing from my mother for the children to travel home in. In his top coat, trousers and socks Marcus no longer looked like our small boy. It already takes long enough for him to dress, with or without help – goodness knows how we are going to get on with umpteen layers! Of course Simeon will need every possible layer as he refuses to stay covered up and thinks it's a game to kick off everything immediately. I have come to the conclusion that he can't bear blankets and have ordered for him the thickest possible sleeping bag.

Simeon has progressed amazingly this past month. No digestive upsets and no hernia pain. So it looks as if at long last his troubles are behind him. He has got us all completely under his thumb and knows it. But he's so hard to resist! Even Marcus can't ignore him when he screams with laughter and blows bubbles or, as Marcus says, "spits a lot" and just asks for attention. John says he is his biggest time-waster in Aitutaki!

This sounds as if Marcus is being pushed out but far from it. He sees to that. Several people recently have told me that Marcus has invited them in to see his beautiful baby – we think it's rather sweet of him.

Marcus spent the day with the Witherses recently. Usually when he goes there, they get him to say grace but this time Charles Withers said it. This is Marcus's version of what he said, "God bless our serviettes!" We found out later that the true version was, "Bless this food and us to Thy service".

SHORTAGE OF WATER

We are now well and truly in the dry season and keeping our fingers crossed for rain. One tank is empty and the larger one has roughly eight inches left. Nearly all our water gets used twice over one way or another. Dirty lettuce water soaks dirty saucepan. Simeon's bath water (never very bad) soaks his nappies. Water for heating his bottle then cleans it, etc. However, our morale will decline only when we can make no more cups of tea!

Actually is has been trying to rain for several days, though nothing happens. The local people say it will be a few days yet before anything worthwhile comes. All the village tanks are empty and the people are using muddy well water, but it doesn't seem to worry them much. Their attitude to tank water is, "We use what we can today in case we are not here to use it tomorrow!!" Our house girl thinks we are plain daft to go to the lengths we do to preserve our water. She probably wouldn't if she ever had to carry a few bucketfuls up hill for 200 yards or so. However, I doubt if it will come to that!

Simeon's cot cover and blanket

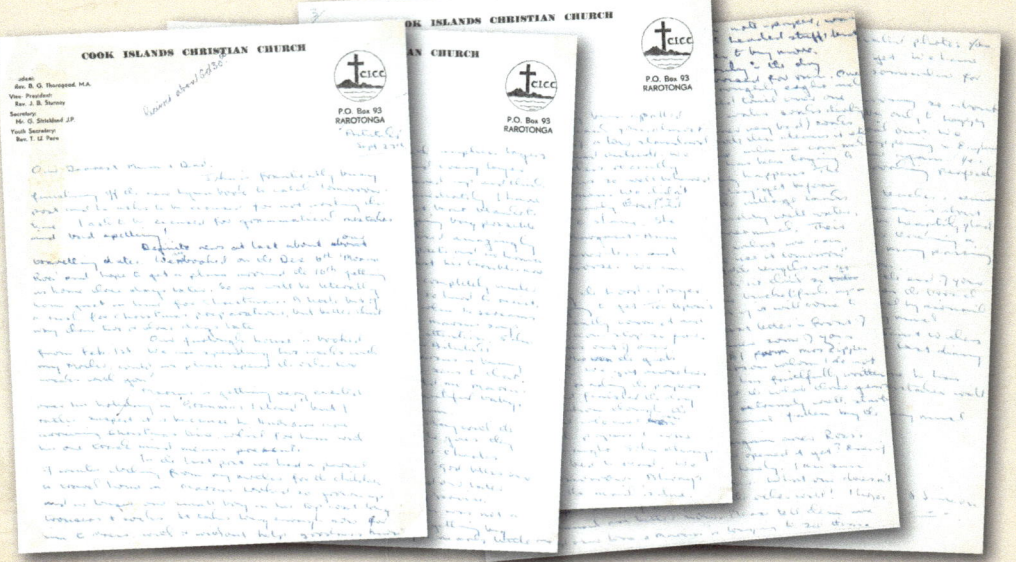

LETTERS FROM OCTOBER 1961 – BUILDINGS GO UP, BUILDINGS COME DOWN

BUILDING A GARAGE

Hymn book typing is all finished now and I'm able to settle down to a more normal life. Which means that with a slightly more humdrum existence there is perhaps not quite so much about which to write. But it's never true to say that life out here is as ordinary and everyday as it often is in England. During the past two days, for instance, I've turned to labouring! The Tautu Church folk have been finishing off the garage which we've attached to the store room (which used to be an outside kitchen). Tautu and Vaipae church people had put up low walls weeks ago but the builders of the Arutanga pastor's new house next door had begun to crack them by using the walls not only as a bench for resting but also for their hammering and sawing. So I got the Tautu pastor to organise things. Some days before the work was done three large packing cases from a local store arrived for the walls. Sounds dreadful, but actually the work has been done very well, and it looks good enough.

Tautu Church

Vaipae Church

FEET INSTEAD OF HANDS

I was watching one of the lads sawing a piece of wood today and it really was an education in the use of poor neglected toes. He balanced the wood on a case, pressed on the overhanging edge he was cutting whilst holding everything firmly in place by his foot. When the wood got too short to hold with his whole foot he simply moved it along until he was only holding on by his big toe!

The pastor's house next door is growing quickly, with the usual army of workmen on Tuesday and Friday mornings. At first they said it would all be finished by October but later they changed the month to November. And now I'm only hoping they'll be finished before we come home.

VILLAGE HALL TAKES 13 YEARS TO BUILD

We have a big day next week with the opening and dedication of the new Arutanga Village Hall. This has been in the process of building for about 12 or 13 years so you can imagine the sort of celebrations that will be held. Plenty of people have told us little bits of the day's happenings – among them that Rita was to take part, cutting the ribbon – but it's only today that we have been presented with an official invitation, on which it states quite clearly what we both have to do.

19TH OCTOBER

9am	All villages present in front of New Hall to receive their share of food prepared by Arutanga people.
12pm	Feast at Sunday School Hall.
1.30pm	All stand in front of New Hall steps. Speaker (Village). Cut Ribbon by R.A. Boys' Brigade will play National Anthem. Key Main door by Mrs. Rev. Sturney.
2pm	Thanks Giving Service control by Rev. Sturney & Pastors. Round imene eight villages start by Amuri. Ureia. Arutanga. Reureu. Nik. Tautu. Vipae. Vaipeka.
3.30pm	Closing. All outside each village form together and show an Item Start by Arutanga. Amuri. Vaipeka. Vaipae. Tautu. Nik. Reureu. Ureia.
7pm	Uapou. Control by Au Orometua. Round Imene start by Vaipae. Tautu. Nik. Reureu. Arutanga. Ureia. Amuri. Vaipeka.
10.30pm	Closing.

20TH OCTOBER

7pm	Free Dance.
10.30pm	Closing by National Anthem.

We know that there will be a huge feast, with plenty of dancing and other items. The family on the other side of us have had most of Arutanga village at their home these past few nights practising. The drums have banged and one song has been sung over and over again. We jolly well ought to know it soon!

FIRE DESTROYS SCHOOL BUILDING

Last Sunday, after the English service, we were having our usual coffee nightcap when, at 10.30pm, the church bell rang vigorously – about 20 persistent strokes. That's the usual fire warning, so we went on to the verandah to have a look. No sign of any fire but plenty of shouting, and hurricane lamps bobbing around. I went up the road and learnt that in fact a house was on fire. So I went along, dog collar and all, to have a look. It proved to be the main school building which, by the time I arrived, was a blazing inferno. This was the original L.M.S. Aitutaki boarding school, built about 80 years ago – a real pioneer coral and lime building although our own house is older by a good 30 years or more. Swarms of people were there, in all states of dress and undress, most of them having obviously sprung straight up from bed on hearing the alarm. Of course there's no fire service here, but this system works almost as well, for as soon as the church bell is rung every able-bodied man and boy is expected to be on the scene immediately.

Unfortunately nothing could be done with the old building as the wood in the roof was as dry as tinder and the fire simply swept through. But in spite of a strong wind the fire was contained in this one block and didn't have a chance to spread to the other dozen or so thatched classrooms. And no one was hurt which was a great blessing.

In one sense many of us were glad it was destroyed by fire. It was due to be demolished in a year or so to make way for a new school, and we'd rather the elements destroyed it than to see it pulled apart bit by bit. A few of the Maoris are not so happy, though, because they look on fire as being an evil (instead of a cleansing) force, and so are beginning to think of the fire as the due result of some evil done. I shall have to take a Sunday soon, and preach on the text "Our God is a consuming fire"!

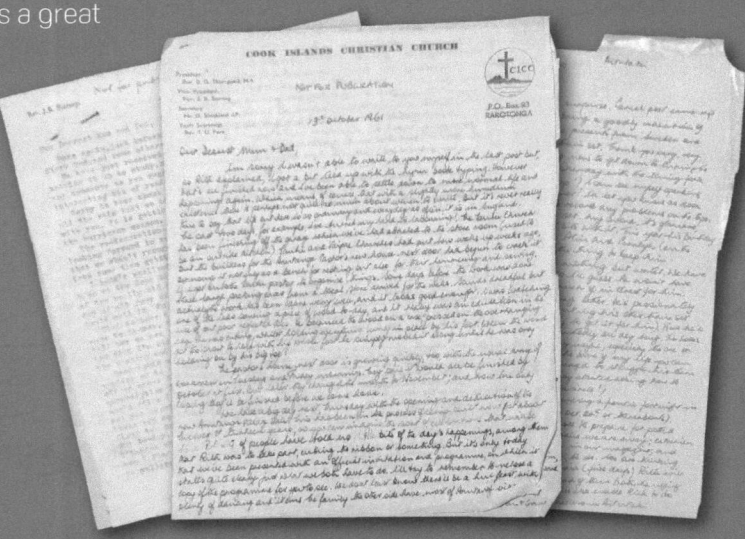

NOVEMBER 1961 – WE SHALL SEE YOU SOON!

OUR ROUTE HOME

This may well be the last letter to reach you before we ourselves arrive. Wonders will never cease to happen; we have heard that the Moana Roa will call at Aitutaki on December 6th, a most unusual call in December as there is virtually no cargo to pick up. We are of course thrilled as it means we won't have the rough ride on a local schooner to Rarotonga first. The ship then goes to Mangaia and from there straight to Auckland. Of course this also means that we won't get to Rarotonga to see the Thorogoods before we leave, which is very disappointing. However, we can't expect too much and are thankful to be picked up here. It also means that although we are only separated from the Thorogoods by 140 miles, they won't see Simeon until he's 15 months old.

We are booked on a plane leaving Auckland. It's only a two-day journey but from all accounts quite a nightmare, stopping at a few places at all odd times. I believe the route is by TEAL to NANDI in Fiji; then by another service to Honolulu, where we stop for about six hours; then on to San Francisco or Chicago; and finally to New York and London. I don't believe we'll be able to leave the Airports without visas. We shall be about finished when we reach London. We are allowed 132 lbs. of luggage but most of that will be Simeon's wardrobe and we're very thankful that we've sent so much stuff off already.

VERY BUSY

Life is now frantically busy. I thought I'd try to take this week off for packing and began on Monday by gaily clearing up my study. Tuesday morning was spent preparing for a farewell party we were running for the Witherses (leaving on the November Moana Roa) and Thorby (Resident Agent) who is leaving with us. Also I had a dental appointment. Wednesday the Witherses had invited us and Mary Hopkirk to one of the islets surrounding the lagoon. Today I've been preparing Sunday School sports for Saturday (celebrating the arrival of the Gospel on Aitutaki). And this afternoon I've had a tooth out – not very pleasant, but the large gap seems to be mending nicely. Tomorrow I shall be writing more last-minute letters and a sermon for Vaipae on Sunday. Then Saturday the sports and farewells to the Witherses. And so I suppose we shall continue till we leave. Fortunately we're pretty fit apart from a cough for Marcus, a nasty sore throat for Rita, and my tooth! Simeon and Marcus play with one another a lot every day, keeping each other in fits of laughter.

In the pages that follow, you will find John's full and unfiltered account of the dramatic first days of Simeon's life – a story of survival against impossible odds. Struggling to take his first breaths on an island where oxygen was scarce, every moment was a battle, every breath a fragile victory. Through John's words, you will witness the desperation, the fear, and the unwavering determination that shaped those critical hours.

WHEN GOD TOOK CONTROL

"John, John, come here quickly!"

The words called through our bedroom door were accompanied by a tatoo of knocking. I tumbled out of bed and found Janet standing outside with a bundle in her arms.

"It's the baby," she whispered – "I must get him down to the hospital; there's something wrong."

The moon shone suddenly lighting up the verandah of our South Sea Island home, and I could see the baby's face, pinched and puckered like a screwed up piece of rag.

"He's stopped breathing!"

But Janet was away, running down the rough stone path across our lawn, stumbling and slipping over the uneven surface. She came to a banana plantation, through which the moon shone weakly, hiding in deep shadow the fallen tree trunks and heavily hanging clusters of bananas. She almost dropped the baby several times in her desperate down-hill flight to the little stone hospital of Aitutaki. How she got there safely is a mystery to her to this day: she had never been that way before. But at last she ran on to the lighted verandah and pushed the baby into the arms of the Cook Island doctor.

Doctor Snowball shook his head in an attitude of resignation. He had seen enough dead babies before to know that there was no exception. But Janet, herself a New Zealand nurse before her marriage, refused to give up so easily.

"Any ideas of what we could do?" Snowball asked.

"Give him adrenalin, and pack him with hot water bottles," Janet suggested.

Within seconds the syringe was stabbed into the little arm by Snowball, and the tiny chest massaged. In a short time he began breathing again fitfully.

"He's going to need oxygen", warned Janet. "I presume you have some here. I know the baby's mother had asked for some to be available in case it was a difficult labour."

Snowball wearily shook his head. "We have no oxygen; the ship did not bring the supplies. We are not expecting another ship for at least ten days."

"Well, he won't live without that," Janet commented in a matter-of-fact way, as she watched the tiny lungs trying hard to raise the chest in expansion.

At that moment I arrived at the hospital having, as I thought, successfully calmed my wife, and tried to hide the panic that must have been in my voice as I told her what was happening whilst getting on a few clothes.

"What about your husband, Janet, at the Airport? Surely he'll have some there."

We were on the phone straightway. The urgency in Janet's voice was contagious, and her husband promised to come immediately with the one and only cylinder that was left at the Airport.

At two o'clock in the morning we were back home, the baby in his pram, an oxygen mask over his face, and a half-empty cylinder lying beside, supplying the life-giving gas, raising and lowering his tiny one-day-old chest.

At first light I went to the Resident Agent to ask for some further supplies of oxygen to be shipped to us immediately.

"You realise, John," he said, as I explained what had been happening in the night, "you realise that, though I can radio immediately for help, it will be at least twenty-four hours before a boat can get here from Rarotonga? And by that time…"

"I know, it may be too late. But surely you can see that at lesat it's worth trying."

"Oh, yes," he replied. "I'll radio them right away. We'll do everything we can. Try not to worry. And do try to stop Rita from getting too upset."

How many times had I told others the same thing! And now in the middle of my own crisis I was told not to worry! I went back home, there was nothing else to do. Rita and I needed each other then as almost at no other time in our married life. We dared not ask Janet or Dr. Snowball what the chances were for our son. It was obvious to everyone that they were very slim. Every now and then a Maori nurse would check the pulse, the oxygen mask, and the all-important needle marking the oxygen remaining in the big metal cylinder. Janet would sit making notes of any changes in his condition; and from time to time, would re-adjust the flow, trying hard to preserve the little oxygen we had left, and yet being careful not to starve him of life. Sometimes he whimpered and was given honey from the end of a tiny spoon.

"He mustn't be allowed to cry," Janet said as she went over to comfort him. "It will weaken him further, and we'll use more oxygen on him."

Sometimes he seemed to be sinking into a coma, and the pressure of oxygen was increased. We stood about helplessly while all this clinical calmness went on around us. I tried to get Rita to go back to bed. She had no business to be up: the baby had only been born 30 hours or so previously, and she should have been resting. But she sat hour after hour, waiting for some change.

At mid-day the Resident Agent called. He asked me to step out on to the verandah, and I knew the news was not good.

"I've been in touch with the Chief Medical Officer on Rarotonga by radio telephone," he said. "He wants to know if you do really want the oxygen."

I was stunned for a moment that such a question could even be asked. Then I realised that perhaps the C.M.O. had diagnosed something that might leave a permanent scar, or that was progressively worsening. All these thoughts came crowding in as I stood trying to answer the Resident Agent.

"Naturally I want oxygen," I stammered. "At least let's give him a fighting chance for survival."

"I thought you'd say that," the R.A. replied. "In fact I said the same thing to the C.M.O. myself. But I thought I had better just check with you that that was right."

Others on the Island were beginning to hear about the baby and were as kind in their own way as the Resident Agent had just been. They brought large bunches of bananas, kumara, yam, in the hope that their gifts and good wishes, their presents and prayers might save the baby's life – their baby, as they already called him.

Rita slept fitfully as the day lengthened and the tropical night fell suddenly. We kept our spirits up by trying to work out when the ship was likely to arrive, assuming always that in this kind of emergency a boat would have been sent immediately. At eight o'clock the Resident Agent returned. I took a spitting oil lamp into my study and we sat together grimly avoiding each other's innermost thoughts. The prospects were worse than I had expected.

"They've no trading schooner at Rarotonga at present, I'm afraid," said the R.A.

"But they must have," I replied. "Where are they all?"

"Out and round the Group somewhere. The nearest is about 500 miles to the north. But there is one hope. A small pleasure yatch has just arrived in Rarotonga from New Zealand. It seems that it has had a battering coming up here and the engine has broken down. But the Public Works Department has promised to set it right as soon as they can."

"What about the crew?"

"Oh, they're all right. They agreed to sail the moment they heard of our trouble. But there's no point in coming under sail only, they'd never get here!"

At last we had something to hold on to. But whether we dared to hope that they would arrive with the precious cargo of oxygen before our supply ran out, no one could tell. Janet's husband looked at the dials on the cylinder thoughtfully, and said that the supply should last if we could cut it off from time to time. Later still I looked at the dials and at my watch trying to calculate which would arrive first: death from an empty cylinder, or new bottled life. But it was a ridiculous, stupid thing to try to calculate something like that because I had left God out of the equation.

I began to try to pray as I had never prayed before. I went on the verandah steps and found myself promising God all sorts of things; bargening with Him, cajoling Him, exhorting Him to give and not to take life away. I went indoors broken in spirit, and in despair.

The next day was one of the worst I have ever known. The baby was more fretful than ever, weaker, his breathing more and more laboured. Our tempers were frayed from lack of sleep. And when Dr. Snowball accidentally knocked the rubber feed tube from the cylinder and allowed much of the precious gas to escape under tremendous pressure all over the room, we almost accused him of murder! None of us could eat. We just drank endless cups of coffee with which the housegirl kept us uncomplainingly supplied.

Rita and I tried to face up to things as they came, but it was not easy. We had fought for what seemed an eternity, and all to so little purpose. We had sat for hours long into the night beside the hissing parafin lamp, which flickered and waned at times almost in harmony with the shallow laboured breaths from the pram. We had paced up and down the verandah screwing up our eyes against the setting sun for the first sign of a sail. Now it seemed to be all over. The Lord gave, and the Lord was going to take away. I suddenly wondered whether or not I should baptise the baby. But it seemed such an extreme act of faithlessness, and really so unnecessary.

The Resident Agent suddenly appeared on the verandah, out of the darkness, breathless with the first good news for days.

"The yatch – Tempest – is almost ready, and should leave at first light."

He was so pleased with his news; yet we could raise so little enthusiasm. We knew now that we had to wait another 24 hours before we could really begin to hope. The crossing normally took 16 hours, but that was in a larger vessel than a yatch.

The next day passed. The housegirl brought in occasional meals, which we picked at and left. Snowball stayed for several hours, but had his other patients to visit. The Maori nurse left behind looked bewildered by all the fuss over a dying baby. Janet encouraged and even bullied us into some kind of activity, even if it was only conversation.

When night fell the Resident Agent sent word that the Government launch was standing by ready to dash across the reef to bring the oxygen and a doctor, who was also coming, ashore the minute the yatch appeared. I sat on the verandah and watched the searchlights of the launch wandering backwards and forwards across the reef, and beyond, trying hopefully to attract the yatch to its beam.

As I sat I thought of the people who had been spending their time worrying about a dying baby, and the people who even now were risking their lives for this little scrap of humanity. There were men out there in the launch in immediate danger of being swept on to the reef in the darkness and crushed by their own boat. And there was the crew of the Tempest, complete strangers to us, battling their way through the continual white horses of the Pacific.

Suddenly I realised that if these people were concerned like this then how much more concerned must God be. I had tried to tell God what to do. I had tried to keep all the worry to myself, thinking that perhaps He was weighing things up, before deciding whether to give or to take life. Then I knew that He was far more concerned and worried and troubled about our baby than ever I would be. So I put it all in His hands, not with an air of resignation, but of trust. I had to let God do the caring, for He was much better at it than I was. All the anxiety of the past few days, the sickening fear, the terrible helplessness of standing by watching a baby fight for every breath was all gone. It was as if God took it from me, and said: "This is My worry, not yours. Let Me bear it now. Let Me take control."

I slept peacefully, out on the verandah, knowing that every thing was being taken care of; it was all out of my hands. The next afternoon at three o'clock the Tempest struggled across the reef. It had taken her 30 hours to cover 150 miles! The crew had forced every mile out of her unwilling engine, feeling at times that they would never make it; and then knowing themselves to be driven relentlessly over the next wave and the next and the next. The doctor stepped ashore, climbed swiftly up the hill to our house, looked at the baby, and switched off the oxygen! After a momentary struggle the baby took his first breath of fresh South Sea Island air, gasped and cried, filling his little lungs over and over again with pure sweetness. Some of us cried too.

He is now eight years old, and has suffered no real effects whatsoever from that day to this, in fact from the very moment when God took control.

WHAT HAPPENED NEXT – SIMEON

During our time on furlough in the UK, Dad and Mum spoke to various groups about their work in the islands and met with members of the L.M.S., as well as spending time with family and friends. In mid 1962 we returned to the Cook Islands, staying in Aitutaki. During his time working alongside the Rev. Bernard Thorogood, Dad had been the Vice President of the Cook Island Christian Church and very much his junior. However, when Bernard Thorogood left the Islands, we had already moved to Rarotonga and Dad took over as the Principal of Takamoa Theological College, until Bernard's replacement came. Dad loved his time in the islands, especially his work with various student groups – both in Aitutaki and Rarotonga.

In 1964 Dad and Mum decided it was time for them to go back to England. Mum, Marcus and I returned to England at the end of the year and Dad, who was reluctant to leave, followed in 1965. At the end of that year my sister – Jennifer was born. Dad then felt the call to go into teaching and duly retrained, specialising in Religious Education. This began a twenty-five-year career in teaching. Dad was also regularly preaching in various churches. Eventually he gave up teaching and went back into full-time ministry overseeing churches, firstly in south-west London and then on the south coast in Dorset, UK. Prior to marrying Dad, Mum had trained as a nursery nurse. During a twenty-year period she ran three playgroups, she loved working with children. Upon his retirement from full-time ministry, Dad became a chaplain at a hospice for the terminally ill. It was during this time that Mum died, 2004.

As for us – the children: Marcus has had a successful career in Town and Country Planning, as a planning officer and more recently a planning consultant. He still enjoys exploring but not so much barefoot these days, and would love to get back to the islands again. I'm currently a prison chaplain and author, married to Julie for over 40 years, with two children: Kathryn married to Andy, with two children of their own, and Daniel married to Ruari. Jennifer is now a dedicated grandma with three children – Lucy, Katie and Alex and she has two grandchildren. She still dreams of visiting the islands for the first time.

After Mum's death Dad, along with Marcus and his partner Verity, visited the islands for the first time since Dad had left. I had taken my family to visit the islands two years earlier. Sometime later Dad married Carole and took her to see the islands. Carole has family is New Zealand and they have holidayed there a few times.

Over the years we have constantly thought about the islands. However, the L.M.S. had a policy that once a missionary left their post, they were not to have contact with the people they once ministered. That didn't stop Dad from being asked to talk about his time in the islands – this went on for years. They also brought back various artefacts from their time in the Cook Islands and I have been the custodian of these for many years. Some of our artefacts are on display in the Cook Islands Library and Museum, near Takamoa in Rarotonga.

The family, including Dad and Mum's grandchildren and great-grandchildren, all know of our connection with the islands and my daughter was married on One Foot Island, Aitutaki. In this age of social media and high-speed communication we have many friends from the Cook Islands, including some who still remember my parents when they lived there. My family and I have been back a few times. I have had the privilege of preaching in the Arutanga CICC where I was christened and seeing the house and room I was born in.

At the time of writing this Dad is still very active. We talk regularly about the islands and Carole follows what is happening in the Cook Islands via social media and updates Dad. He is still interested in following what the Cook Island Christian Church is doing and in 2021 he sent them his greetings when they celebrated the 200th anniversary of the arrival of the first missionaries.

PERSONAL REFLECTIONS – SIMEON

It wasn't until adulthood that I became fully aware of the uniqueness of my situation, someone born in the Cook Islands but not a Cook Islander. Yes, I was born to the rhythm of the waves crashing against the reef, the swaying of the palm trees and the singing and dancing of the islanders, a very different rhythm to the one I'm used to in the UK. Of course I had no choice in where I was born; and as I don't have Kuki Airani DNA in me, I'm not legally a Cook Islander. Yet I'm extremely proud of my birthplace and very happy to be called by locals a "Rutang boy", a boy of the village of Arutanga, Aitutaki. But, however you view it, I'm a papa'a – a "white" person. *Papa'a* refers to four garments of clothing – vest, shirt, waistcoat and jacket, the clothing early white men wore when they first arrived. Yet no one can take my birth certificate away, or the fact that I have New Zealand and British passports that say I was born in the Cook Islands. And every time I leave the house I carry the Cook Islands with me – my place of birth is stated on my driving licence.

My birthplace has brought challenges. Several years ago I was going through the vetting process to become a volunteer chaplain in an immigration removal centre. Filling in the extensive documentation I put my birthplace down. I was then asked by those processing the information to produce my "right to remain" documentation, which I didn't have. For nearly 72 hours the

Home Office believed I could be in the UK illegally. The irony was that I was close to being offered a bed in the detention centre, rather than keys as volunteer chaplain, it was pretty scary. Thankfully I had Mum's old passport which showed I was added on in 1961. And as someone who finds spelling a challenge at the best of times, can you imagine growing up trying to spell Aitutaki. As an eight-year-old I remember having to write a paragraph titled 'Where I was born'. I remember being surprised the teacher didn't know how to spell it either. We settled on me writing "the Cook Islands".

I'm often asked why I'm living in the UK and not the islands. There are several reasons, one being the lengthy process I would need to go through to gain permanent residency, which would obviously include living there all year round. However, the main reason is because my family are in the UK. My wife and I have our children and their families here. Of course both our daughter and son have New Zealand passports and could reside in New Zealand and potentially live in the Cook Islands if they were given PR but neither are minded to at the moment. Yet from a young age they were told of their connection with the islands and we have been able to visit Kuki Airani as a family on a couple of occasions. Our grandchildren are also aware of their connections.

As a family, whenever we have the chance to support the Cook Islands, especially in sport, we do. My son-in-law is a very keen rugby league fan. The family have been to a few rugby league World Cup matches in the UK, supporting the Cook Islands. We were at one match in Wales watching the Cook Islands take on the home nation, and beat them. At half time I got talking to some other Cook Island supporters – we were very much in the minority. They were watching their son play and had travelled from New Zealand. Of course they asked me why I was supporting the islands. When I told them I was born in Aitutaki, the man said that his late uncle had lived there – he had been a doctor. I looked at him and asked what his name was, his reply: "Dr. Snowball". Here I was, standing in a stadium in Wales, UK, next to the nephew of the man who helped save my life! It was the first time I had been able to thank a member of the Snowball family for the actions of Dr Snowball. Since then I have met his daughter and other family members. Hopefully one day I'll meet the family of Janet Withersses and thank them for her part in saving my life.

PERSONAL REFLECTIONS — KATHRYN (SIMEON AND JULIE'S DAUGHTER)

When I was a child, I would often dream aloud about holidaying in Barbados. My dad's response was always the same: "Why Barbados and not the Cook Islands?" This question sparked my curiosity about the Cook Islands and what they had to offer. These early conversations made me aware of my connections to the Cook Islands and the reason why I held a New Zealand passport.

The first time I stepped onto the sand at Muri Beach, Rarotonga, as an 18-year-old is a moment I will always remember. It was then that I finally understood the dream my dad had been trying to share with me for so many years. During my first visit to Rarotonga and Aitutaki, I learnt more about our unique family history, visiting the house my dad was born in and meeting family friends.

The beauty of the islands was overwhelming, and I knew I wanted to return one day. This heritage became even more significant when I married Andy on One Foot Island, Aitutaki, in 2012. Andy has enthusiastically embraced our family history and connection to the islands, supporting us to realise our dream of being married there and making new connections during this visit.

Eleven years later (20 years after my first visit), we returned with our children to share the culture and history of the islands with them, and of course to show them the incredible *motu* we were married on. We attended church services and cultural shows, played football with younger generations of our friends' family, and even had a traditional dance lesson on the beach. Attending the church where my dad was christened, hearing the rich harmonies of the congregation, and thinking about how my grandparents may have felt to be in the same church many years ago was incredibly special. Seeing my dad preach at the sunrise service, just as my grandpa would have done, was a poignant moment for me.

Our children have grown up knowing they have a connection to the Cook Islands, just as I did. They have been privileged to visit the islands with their grandparents, seeing where their great-grandpa lived and worked on both Rarotonga and Aitutaki, and where their grandad was born and christened. Meeting and reconnecting with people who knew our family when they originally lived there has added another layer of connection, which we hope our children will continue to build upon, to strengthen the legacy of their great-grandparents' mission.

As a family, we have supported both the men's and women's Cook Islands rugby league teams at several World Cup Final matches in the UK, proudly waving the Cook Islands flag and wearing our rugby shirts, scarves and *Ei Katu* (flower head garland). We now have our own Cook Islands memorabilia from our visits and from supporting the rugby league teams. After hearing the beautiful Cook Islands National Anthem sung at the Rugby League World Cup finals, I was eager to experience it again during our visit to the islands in 2023, and I was not disappointed. On New Year's Eve, while walking on the sand with my dad and children, we stumbled upon locals singing the same anthem in the dark, with the moon rising above Muri Beach – the very place where I first discovered the islands' beauty.

EPILOGUE – SIMEON

"Wonderfully Made"

There is a Psalm in the Bible (Psalm 139), where the author David writes about himself as being "fearfully and wonderfully made". I can relate to that, especially when I think of all the life experiences I've had which have shaped and made me who I am today. None more so than being born on Aitutaki, Cook Islands / Kuki Airani. However, as not being of Maori descent I'm not considered a Cook Islander. Sadly, I left the islands before I could speak fluently and therefore never learnt the language. As I don't have any Cook Island heritage, I don't own any land. So to many islanders I would be viewed as a foreigner. It is extremely important to the islanders that they limit outsiders' influences, as they strive to maintain their traditions, culture and language, so only those with Kuki Airani heritage are legally Cook Islanders. To this day they are determined to maintain their control on their land and are understandably cautious when striking agreements with other countries.

Many visitors to the islands are immediately struck by how beautiful they are, each with its own character, all wonderfully made. Yet as my Mum and Dad's letters show, everyday living can be a very different experience to that of a visitor, and of course times change. It is lovely to have an account of three of the six years we lived in the South Pacific, over 60 years ago. A lot has changed since then, especially regarding the infrastructure – houses, roads, transport and of course communication. But many of the customs and traditions remain the same.

However, there is another difference that is having an impact on the islands, some of which are atolls, and that is climate change. As sea levels rise, some of the lower-lying islands are increasingly under threat, especially during cyclone season – when wind and tidal surges can wreak havoc and devastation. Water shortages are also becoming more common. Other challenges to the way of life in the islands is the cost of living, as so much has to be imported. Tourism, although it brings in much-needed finance, its "footprint" in terms of pressure on the resources is becoming an issue.

Some of the missionaries brought their own culture and perspective on how life should be lived. Thankfully, traditional singing, dancing and storytelling remain strong. I'm so proud of Dad because he learnt Rarotongan Maori and could read, write as well as speak it fluently – he knew the importance of respecting the islands culture. Among the Christians on Aitutaki today there is a story that a prophecy was given to the main tribal leader, the Ariki, that said people were coming to bring them news about 'God'. So when the very first missionaries – John Williams and Papeiha – arrived in 1821 they were welcomed openly by the Ariki, and understandably the rest of the people followed the Ariki's lead. Today the people of the islands still welcome guests, but of course there is an expectation that in return the guests respect the islands, their culture, faith and land. There is a belief that the islanders don't own the land but that the land owns those born on it. I feel so blessed to be owned by the land of Arutanga, Aitutaki, Kuki Airani, a land that is wonderfully made and dedicates itself to God.

What's your legacy?

GALLERY

TAUTA PASTOR PACKING TOMATOES

PANDANUS TREE – LEAVES USED FOR THATCHING

OVEN FOR BAKING BREAD

BREAD BOY BLOWING CONCHE SHELL TO ANNOUNCE ARRIVAL

TOMATO SHIPPING DAY AT WHARF

TYPICAL MAORI HUT

RECENTLY BUILT STORE

TYPICAL ADMINISTRATION BUILT HOUSE

MAIN VAIPAE-TAUTU ROAD – VAIPAE PASTOR RETURNING FROM PLANTATION WORK

TYPICAL MAORI KITCHEN

MAORI HUT BEING BUILT

ADMINISTRATION OFFICE

HUSKING COCONUTS

MARCUS IN THE GARDEN

MARCUS WITH FRIENDS

MARCUS

MARCUS WITH FRIENDS

JOHN, RITA, MARCUS & SIMEON

DANCING

BEACH AT AMURI 1960

BEACH AT AMURI 2023

CHILDREN IN HUT

AKAIAMI MOTU – LANDING STAGE FOR SEAPLANE

ONE FOOT ISLAND 2023

LOCAL WOMEN & CHILDREN

SCHOOL CHILDREN

RITA & TAKAMOA STUDENTS

RITA & TAKAMOA WOMEN

LOCAL WOMEN & CHILDREN

SIMEON

RITA & SIMEON

MARCUS'S BIRTHDAY

MARCUS'S BIRTHDAY

MARCUS, SIMEON & FRIENDS

MARCUS HELPING OUT

FISHING

MARCUS & SIMEON

MARCUS, SIMEON & FRIENDS

RITA, MARCUS & SIMEON

THE STURNEY FAMILY RETURN TO AITUTAKI

LOCAL CHILDREN

JOHN, RITA, MARCUS & SIMEON WITH PAGE – NZ JOURNALIST AND FRIEND

THE STURNEY COLLECTION FOUND IN THE LIBRARY & MUSEUM, RAROTONGA

JOHN & RITA

THE STURNEY FAMILY

THE STURNEY COLLECTION FOUND IN THE LIBRARY & MUSEUM, RAROTONGA

THE STURNEY COLLECTION FOUND IN THE LIBRARY & MUSEUM, RAROTONGA

THE ONCE STURNEY AITUTAKI HOME 2023

SIMEON, JULIE, KATHRYN & DANIEL

SIMEON WITH DR SNOWBALL'S FAMILY

SIMEON PREACHING IN ARUTANGA CICC

RAROTONGA CICC

JULIE, SIMEON, RUAIRI & DANIEL

THE STURNEY FAMILY TODAY WITH THEIR PARTNERS

JOHN & MARCUS

JOHN & SIMEON

JOHN & HIS DAUGHTER JEN

JOHN & CAROLE

Copyright © Simeon Sturney 2025

First published 2025 by Sarah Grace Publishing, an imprint of Malcolm Down Publishing Ltd.

www.malcolmdown.co.uk

29 28 27 26 25 7 6 5 4 3 2 1

The right of Simeon Sturney to be identified as the author of this work has been asserted by him in accordance with the Copyright, Designs and Patents Act 1988.

All rights reserved. No part of this publication may be reproduced, stored in a retrieval system, or transmitted in any other form or by any means, electronic, mechanical, photocopying, recording or otherwise, without the prior permission of the publisher.

British Library Cataloguing in Publication Data
A catalogue record for this book is available from the British Library.

ISBN 978-1-917455-21-3

Design by Faye Porter
Art direction by Sarah Grace
Printed in the UK